DUSTY

ASTROLOGY'S
HIDDEN ASPECTS

QUINTILES AND
SESQUIQUINTILES

REDFeather
MIND | BODY | SPIRIT

Copyright © 2018 by Dusty Bunker

Library of Congress Control Number: 2017955755

Designed by Brenda McCallum
Type set in Copperplate/Times

ISBN: 978-0-7643-5543-1
Printed in China

Published by Red Feather Mind, Body, Spirit
An imprint of Schiffer Publishing, Ltd
4880 Lower Valley Road
Atglen, PA 19310
Phone: (610) 593-1777; Fax: (610) 593-2002
E-mail: Info@schifferbooks.com
Web: www.schifferbooks.com

For our complete selection of fine books on this and related subjects, please visit our website at www.schifferbooks.com. You may also write for a free catalog.

Schiffer Publishing's titles are available at special discounts for bulk purchases for sales promotions or premiums. Special editions, including personalized covers, corporate imprints, and excerpts, can be created in large quantities for special needs. For more information, contact the publisher.

We are always looking for people to write books on new and related subjects. If you have an idea for a book, please contact us at proposals@schifferbooks.com.

ACKNOWLEDGMENTS

Thanks go to my friend, astrologer Mike Levesque, whose enthusiasm, encouragement, insights, and conversations are a treasure.

Thanks as always to the people at Red Feather for their professionalism and support. Their artistry creates the jewels that make my books glow.

Many thanks to Pete Schiffer for the 6,000 stickers!

And last, but always first, thanks to my family, my greatest treasure of all.

A mathematical equation stands forever.

—Albert Einstein

Almost all the ancient names of Deity,
when their letters are resolved into numbers,
are found to consist of what are sometimes called 'cosmic
numbers' in that they express some great planetary or
terrestrial cycles.

—Ancient Freemasonry, Frank C. Higgins,
(1916) 33rd degree Mason

Geometry has two great treasures:
one is the Theorem of Pythagoras, the other,
the division of a line into extreme and mean ratio.
The first we may compare to a measure of gold;
the second we may name a precious jewel.

—Johannes Kepler (1571–1630)

CONTENTS

CONTENTS

PREHISTORY

An amazing incident occurred very early in my life. Although it happens to all school children, this event had a profound and lasting impact on me.

To set the stage, this was many years ago, before television, kindergarten, and the early learning tools available to children today. I could not read at that point.

I was five years old. I was sitting at my wooden desk with the ink bottle sunk in the upper right corner and the wooden pen handle with the metal tip seated in the groove beside it. I was in the first grade classroom, holding a book, intently studying a colorful picture of Dick and Jane and their little dog, Spot, wondering what the strange glyphs at the bottom of the page meant. As I struggled, suddenly it all came together.

See Spot run.

I was stunned! A wave of power swept from the crown of my head down over my body. It was an alive, palpitating moment, what I can only describe as my soul expanding and extending beyond my physical body. In my child's mind, I recognized I had touched something sacred, something that could change my world.

I could read!

At that moment, at five years old, I knew my destiny. I would read books and I would write books filled with this power that had just filled my soul so that others would know its transforming ecstasy. I would search the mysteries of the universe so that I would know.

I had discovered the power of the Word.

That feeling has never left me.

I had never been able to sufficiently explain this intense transforming experience or my subsequent dedication and immersion for years in the quest for knowledge until the discovery of the golden bowls, the quintile and sesquiquintile.

My Mercury in Scorpio in the Fourth House indicates researching intensely into the roots of subjects, and my Moon in Sagittarius in the Fifth House, suggests a love of knowledge. But, as a Scorpio, I was disappointed that my Mercury was not in aspect to Pluto because I felt the intensity of that association in every fiber of my being. It didn't seem enough that Mercury was in Scorpio, which is ruled by Pluto.

On November 2, 1987, around 10:00 in the morning, while riding home from our cabin on Conner Pond in the hills of New Hampshire, I found my answer. It was a moment of intense emotional contact with the roots of my consciousness. The pieces became the whole. That moment of revelation opened the door to a cupboard filled with rare ingredients.

I realized that I have Mercury sesquiquintile Pluto! It was my turn to cry "Eureka!"

And I did.

At that moment in time, my husband, comfortable with my idiosyncratic manner of dealing with life, merely smiled and asked, "Now what?" Since he is used to waking at 2:30 in the morning to find me on the floor in the dark, bent over an array of books with a flashlight in hand, he takes much of my behavior in stride.

My eureka moment in the car that day came after years of research and study. That moment revealed the intense importance of the little used or understood 72 degree quintile and its partner, the 108 degree sesquiquintile.

Readers of the original edition of this book published in 1989, will recall that, at that time, I called the 108 degree aspect the tredecile. There was and still is confusion even today about the naming of this aspect; it has been called the tredecile, tridecile, and sesquiquintile. However, because of its cosmic roots and after researching the meaning of the word, I believe sesquiquintile is the correct name for the 108 degree aspect. I even like how the word "sesquiquintile" rolls off the tongue. "Sesquiquintile" is a tongue twister, so sometimes I call it the "sesqui."

With the discovery of my natal Mercury sesquiquintile Pluto, I also realized that, when I was five years old and had discovered the power of the word, the progressed Sun was transiting that aspect in my natal chart! I had found the intense connection I was looking for.

The point here is that this electrifying experience was never explained to my satisfaction through examining the traditional aspects in my natal astrological chart. I had wondered about this missing link since I began studying metaphysics in general and astrology in particular.

The discovery of the importance of the quintile and sesquiquintile aspects was the result of many years of studying and contemplating sacred geometry and the principles of numbers. It was through these two "languages" that I realized the importance of this pair of aspects, what the early Egyptians called the "sacred golden bowls."

Because I found overwhelming proof that the quintile and sesquiquintile should be considered the most important aspects in the astrological chart, I wrote that original version of this book in the late 1980s, under the title *Quintiles and Tredeciles*.

I took heart then from the renowned astrologer Carl Payne Tobey, who once wrote: "Our greatest fear is that students will accept only what we have done till now and then get into a rut."[1]

It is now thirty years later and recently, on a lazy summer day in 2016, I was sprawled out in my recliner on the sun porch reading a mystery when the phone rang. It was my publisher, Pete Schiffer. He asked if I had any books in the works. I mentioned I was working on a beginner's book for astrologers.

Then . . . almost as an aside, he asked if I had thought about updating *Quintiles and Tredeciles*. That simple question resulted in this book.

Upon finishing and turning in the manuscript for the astrology book in December of that year, I sat down at my computer on December 12, 2016, and began the process of rewriting the first part of this book. I noted the time that I typed the first few sentences. Later that day I ran off a chart to compare the moment I began to rewrite this book to the chart of my moment of discovery on that ride home from the hills of New Hampshire in November 1987. (Please see the accompanying charts on pages 10 and 11.

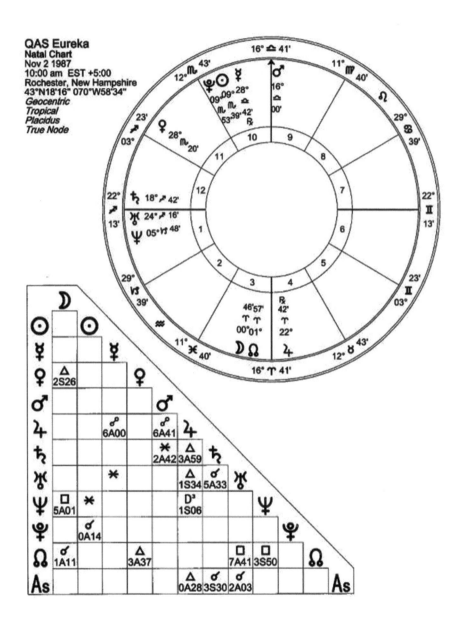

QAS Eureka
Natal Chart
Nov 2 1987
10:00 am EST +5:00
Rochester, New Hampshire
43°N18'16" 070°W58'34"
Geocentric
Tropical
Placidus
True Node

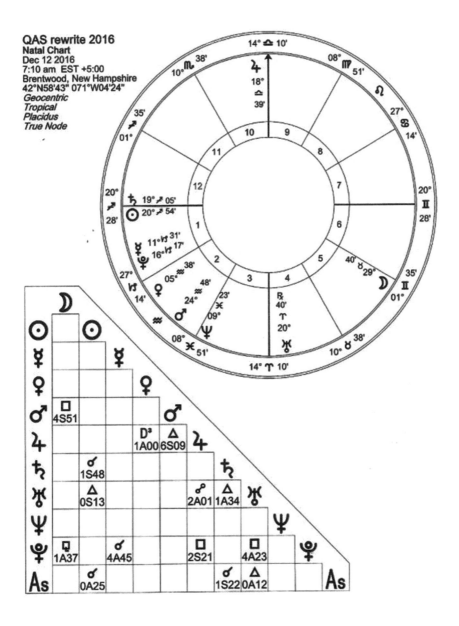

QAS rewrite 2016
Natal Chart
Dec 12 2016
7:10 am EST +5:00
Brentwood, New Hampshire
42°N58'43" 071°W04'24"
Geocentric
Tropical
Placidus
True Node

I shouldn't have been surprised to find major connections between the two charts:

> First: it was the Saturn return, within one degree, of my Eureka moment in 1987.
>
> Secondly: in both charts, Saturn was just above the same Sagittarian ascendant within 2 degrees of each other.
>
> And finally: the Ascendant in both charts is within range of my natal Moon.

I mean, how weird is that! My planetary guardians must have been shouting in my ears for months. Since I didn't hear their message, they decided to contact me through my publisher. The universe does know what it's doing.

While rewriting this book I slowly realized that, through my years as an astrologer working with these aspects, I had gained an understanding of how they operate in the natal chart. As a result, in this book you will find my interpretations of the quintile and sesquiquintile using the traditional ten "planets" and the Ascendant. As far as I know, this is the first time this has been done.

A note to you who do not have the quintile and sesquiquintile aspects in your natal chart: You may already know what your talents are, and you may have already recognized the path you will take this lifetime. Your focus is not on defining these objectives, but rather your focus is on using your energy, drive, and determination to achieve these objectives. You're already on your way.

So, now my friends, as the six-year old boy said to my husband when he was leading a tour group through our local Great Bay Estuary and had evidently stopped at an instructional site for too long, "Can we move on?"

Yes, it's time to move on . . .

The previous edition of this book came out in 1989, when my manuscript was written on a portable typewriter. At that time, there was no Internet for public use like we have today; the Internet was in use around the early 1980s, in universities and labs, and perhaps earlier in the military, but all I had was my portable typewriter, my own library, and visits to the public library.

My experience with the quintile and sesquiquintile was the result of using information I had gathered over twenty years by studying esoteric numbers and sacred geometry, through gematria (the practice of calculating the numeric equivalent of words and phrases by adding up the numbers associated with each letter), and by studying old Masonic manuscripts along with religious texts and Egyptian symbols.

I also used my old standbys—a protractor, compass, ruler, and square—to draw various symbols and number combinations on paper; I still have stacks of those old illustrations. This background research and the many consultations I had given to that point added more fuel to the fire of my wondering. I spent many quiet hours back then, pencil chewing, as I gazed into space.

Those hours were precious because, at that time, I had a house full of teenagers who would pop into my quiet corner and say, "Mom . . . since you're not doing anything, would you . . . (fill in the blank). When a mother is motionless, obviously she's not doing anything important. After a respectful conversation and a posted sign that read "Do Not Disturb unless there is a Supernova," we worked it out. Although there *were* some minor supernovae; I'm a mother, after all.

The quintile and sesquiquintile aspects explained something I felt so profoundly that I knew they had to be extremely important. But I was not aware of why or how until I had my "Eureka" moment mentioned earlier.

Through the exercise of the above-mentioned disciplines, the importance of this pair of aspects, the golden bowls, was revealed to me.

First, I realize that the word "sesquiquintile" is a mouthful so, if you prefer, you can think of that word as the 'sesqui' as noted before. Even your mother most likely gave you a nickname different from your given formal name. I mean, who wants to go around being called Penelope Beauregard Cumberbatch, the III. Although I do love the actor Benedict Cumberbatch, especially in the role of Sherlock Holmes! So, if you like the way the word sesquiquintle rolls around in your mouth, by all means use it, but if you get tongue tied trying to pronounce it, like I do, just go with its nickname, sesqui. That's my choice.

Secondly, my discovery of the importance of the quintile and the sesquiquintile went against astrological tradition that describes the quintile as: "a minor aspect introduced by Kepler that combines planets separated by one-fifth of the zodiac, or 72°. The quintile is generally regarded as favorable; it has been associated with both talent and power."[1]

Regardless of the descriptions of these astrological aspects as "minor," "generally favorable," and "mildly beneficial," I discovered that the quintile and its sister the sesquiquintile are the most important aspects in the astrological pantheon because they emerged from the Cosmic Egg! They are cosmic twins. Therefore, they should carry the same family name: quintile.

Thirdly, when I'm typing a manuscript, I leave spaces between paragraphs. This has always been my method. I never thought about why I do this until recently when I heard the musician Sting interviewed. When asked what music was about, he thought for a moment, and then replied, "Music is the silence between the notes."

That simple statement hit me like a lightning bolt! Yes! That is why I leave spaces between my paragraphs! The space between paragraphs allows me as the writer and you as the reader a millisecond to absorb the impact of that thought before moving on to the next paragraph. That gives us both that millisecond to allow that information to seep into our consciousness. We might even stop, go back, and reread that paragraph, and then think more deeply about what that thought evokes in our mind.

This process stimulates the imagination. As Einstein said, "Imagination is more important than knowledge. For knowledge is limited to all we now know and understand, while imagination embraces the entire world, and all there ever will be to know and understand."[2]

And finally, for you fire signs, if you want to first jump ahead to Part III to read the delineations of the ten planets and the Ascendant using the quintile and the sesquiquintile aspects, by all means, go ahead. But after that, please do come back to read Part I, because here you will find the fascinating story behind these two most important aspects in the astrological chart. Plus you will see how I arrived at the meaning of these two essential aspects and thereby discovered the Golden Bowl Rectangle.

So, my friends, it really is time to move on. Enjoy the journey.

PART I

CHAPTER 1

PREPARATION FOR YOUR ARCHAEOLOGICAL EXPEDITION

Time to gather your archaeological tools, your khaki shorts, and your Indiana Jones soft hat; we're about to embark on a journey into the mists of time to uncover the sacred golden bowls . . . the two aspects: the 72°quintile and the 108° sesquiquintile.

In order to follow the map to the treasure site, we need only ten tools.

How awesome is that! It couldn't be much simpler.

Yet, you will also discover that these ten tools are the most powerful in the Universe, because they explain the birth of the cosmos as well as the "birth" of any "thing" in your life, and they will uncover the hidden treasures we seek.

The steps in this journey will be shown so clearly you will be amazed. It's as simple as 1-2-3. Literally. This discovery will knock your sandy socks off!

So, tighten your belt, sling your tool bag over your shoulder, and clamp a hand on your hat as we set out on our trek across the wind-blown desert sands to discover the golden bowls, the quintile and sesququintile, those Cosmic Twins that emerged from the Cosmic Egg, moments after the Big Bang.

Thirsty? Ready to sip from the golden bowls? Okay . . . we're off.

The first five tools in our bag are the numbers 1, 2, 3, 4, and 5.

The ancients viewed numbers from a different perspective than we do today. Their understanding and use of numbers had no relationship to the mathematics we currently use. If we are to understand the teachings of the ancient mystery schools, especially those taught through numbers and sacred geometry, which are the proof offered in this book for the validation of the quintile and sesquiquintile, then we need to examine the way in which these ancients thought about and used numbers.

To these early people, a number was the "extreme reduction of philosophic thought." Each number represented a specific principle.

And the numbers were part of a progressive sequence that explained the formative life processes. Things had to be done by the numbers, in a prescribed order, in order to reach the desired conclusion.

Each number was a universal principle that emerged from the preceding number, and all numbers emerged from the One in an order prescribed by cosmic law.

The ancients believed that the orderly progression of the numbers resulted in time and space and life, and eventually the dissolution of that life, which was then recycled and reborn.

Schwaller de Lubicz, the twentieth-century student of sacred geometry, an Egyptologist known for his years of studying the art and architecture of the Temple of Luxor, which he described in his book, *The Temple in Man*, wrote: " . . . in the ancient temple civilization of Egypt, numbers, our most ancient form of symbols, did not simply designate quantities but instead were considered to be concrete definitions of energetic formative principles of nature."[1]

Pretty heady stuff, right? But it's simple really . . . the numbers represent an energy that works in an orderly set of steps in order to reach a goal.

The ancients saw One as the circle that contained everything, the Cosmic Womb of creation.

They saw Two not as separate from but rather emerging from the One.

This awareness may have resulted from observation of the birth process: a Cosmic Hand did not reach out of the heavens and present the female with a fully formed child to care for. Instead, the woman's body began to expand, like the expanding universe, and at some point, another being emerged from her body. From the Mother, emerged the Child; out of the One emerged the Two.

The very early people, having no concept of the connection between sexual intercourse and the birth of a child nine months later, saw this process as miraculous and, therefore, the woman was considered divine, Earth's representative of the Great Mother who created the universe.

We must remember there is a distinction between figures and numbers. Figures are used to measure how far, how heavy, how many, and how soon. You know, like, "Mom, I need a dozen cupcakes with chocolate frosting for the class party tomorrow morning," and it's 8:30 at night when you're putting your precious little one to bed, and you have no cake mix or frosting in the house, which means a trip to the little country store up the road that closes at 9:00 p.m. Or the boss needs copies in triplicate of the dozen proposals before the eight o'clock board meeting in the morning, and its 6:00 p.m., and you have to pick up the silver engraved anniversary necklace for your mom's big birthday bash at 8:00 across town and you're hoping the jewelers are still open or you'll have to try a little B&E hoping that you don't get caught, and if you do, that the arresting officer will be sympathetic because he has a mom he calls every Sunday.

Once again, as opposed to the figures mentioned above, numbers represent precise principles that, in an orderly progression, created the Universe and all of nature. These principles all emerged from the One.

We use the common expression, "Let's do it by the numbers." What this means is that we should do things in a set of orderly steps in order to be successful at whatever we are attempting to accomplish. The numbers one through nine represent that process. Nothing concrete can be achieved without following these universal steps.

The single numbers One through Nine are the pattern for the universal laws of ebb and flow, which is the natural rhythm of life, much like the ebb and flow of the ocean's tide. These cycles move in a predictable and orderly manner. As one number reaches out to initiate activity, the next number pulls that activity within to nurture and give it substance.

The numbers One through Nine represent one complete process up to the point of recycling matter so that the basic cycle can begin once again.

In this book, we will use the numbers One through Five:

1. One is the beginning, the seed that flows out.
2. Two pulls that energy within to nurture it.
3. Three expands and grows the energy.
4. Four pulls the energy in to give it form.
5. Five animates the form.

This is the process of doing things by the numbers; this is the language of numbers. The birth of the cosmos came about and life operates daily in the same manner.

The second five tools in our bag are the geometric symbols: the vertical line, the horizontal line, the circle, the triangle, and the square.

Not mathematically inclined, I was leery of geometry before I learned the symbolism behind it.

Forget about the geometry we had to endure in high school. Here we are using these five simple geometric symbols that surround us every day. Their subliminal messages are embedded in our society and in our consciousness.

Let's explore the metaphysical symbolism of each one.

> **The vertical line:** energy from above, Cosmic Energy, Spirit:
>
> The vertical line relates to the heavens, the Sun as the Creator, the life-giving force that shines down from above. To the ancients, the vertical line represented the energy that flowed from Heaven into the Earth.
>
> This seems an obvious connection when we realize that, as they gazed into the vast reaches of the night sky where thousands of stars blinked and the planets moved in their eternal patterns, they had to wonder if some great being watched over them. To give meaning to their lives and to connect with a comforting presence who cared for them, they had to believe this was so.
>
> They stretched their arms towards heaven in supplication and prayer to that life-giving force, hoping they could make contact with their Creator, the Great Mother who ruled the universe.

The direction "up" symbolized reaching for that source.

The horizontal line: energy manifested in Matter.

The horizontal line represents space, an abbreviated symbol for the physical world of form, the horizontal plane on which we live and which encompasses all matter, including the human body. Wavy horizontal lines represent the waters of the Earth.

The crossing of the vertical and horizontal lines represents energy from above entering the physical world of form below. The "cross we bear" is the physical body in which we live here on Earth with its accompanying trials and tribulations.

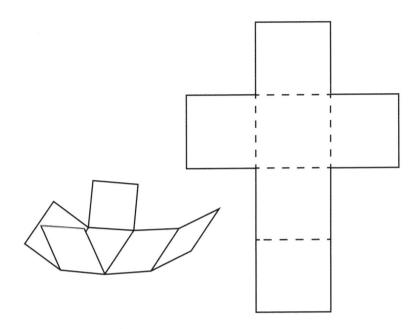

Although, that cross we carry can be light, compassionate, and joyful as we embrace the bounty of this earth.

The point at which the vertical and horizontal lines cross, a 90° angle, is called "the crossing." The crossing is the point where life enters the body, the point of consciousness in the physical world.

The cross is a symbol for Spirit entering Matter.

Take the Christian cross above with the horizontal bar two-thirds of the way up the stem, and fold it inward. It forms a cube, which is the solidified square. The solidified square represents all matter on Earth. Ye are the salt of the Earth, salt crystallizes into cubes.

The cube is the stone that builds the temple. Symbolically, the cross represents the human body, "the temple not built with human hands."

Show and tell—I love it!

Now, on to the circle.

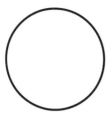

The circle, the Source, the Mother: The circle is the symbol for the Source, the Mother, and the Creator, because it is all encompassing and eternal. The circle contains everything. The circumference of a circle goes round and round and is never ending.

The French philosopher Voltaire wrote about the circle: "God is a circle whose center is everywhere and circumference is nowhere."[2]

You are the center of that circle, the center of your existence because everything you see is around you. Turn 360°; you have created your circle in which you are the center. Your vision is limited by the distance to which you can see.

When you move to another location and turn in a circle, you now have a different vision of the world around you.

As you change your position, the landscape around you changes.

In this sense, your center is everywhere you choose to be; your circumference is nowhere because it changes every time you change your location.

You are the center of the Universe.

Pretty neat, right?

The triangle, Time: The equilateral triangle (three equal sides) symbolizes dynamic energy ready to explode into life.

This triangle expresses the concept of time: past-present-future, beginning-middle-end, mother-father-child, youth-maturity-old age, maiden-mother-crone.

We recognize this trinity through our common expression: things happen in threes. Things do indeed happen in threes, as we shall discover.

The square, Space, Form: The square, and its extension, the cube, are the solid foundations that occupy space. The square represents form and substance, that upon which our physical world is built. Four is the boundaries which enclose those things necessary to ensure the continuance of life.

Think about those honored figures of the past who were called builders, carpenters, and architects. They used their creative energy to erect structures in the physical world of form and substance.

Another look at the circle, the triangle, and the square.

The circle, triangle, and square are reflected even in our handwriting, which stems from our brain/eye/hand coordination, symbols which emerge from our inborn awareness and our early relationship with the world.

The circle is a round soft shape, all encompassing, with no sharp corners. It is the symbol of the Mother Creator. A baby looks up into the round face of those who love her; the breast she suckles is round and soft; her toys have no sharp edges but are round to protect her from harm.

According to handwriting analysis, round-shaped handwriting indicates a person who is motivated by the qualities of nurture, gentleness, and love.

The triangle has sharp corners; it is full of energy and is more daring. A young child who chooses sharp toys to play with is more assertive and daring, unafraid of getting hurt, motivated by the thrill of danger.

Wedge-shaped handwriting suggests an active person who is willing to take chances, who is dynamic and adventurous.

Any squares out there? The square is stable and earthy. In many cases, a toddler sleeps in a modified square crib, his play pen is square; he and his parents live in a house with square rooms; he draws pictures of a square house within which he lives with his family. The square represents security.

Handwriting that looks blocky indicates a person who is down-to-earth, practical, organized, and connected to earthly things, a person who is security conscious.

You will also find that these five geometric symbols—the horizontal line, the vertical line, the circle, the triangle, and the square—evoke the same responses in humans when they are found in buildings, art work, advertising, nature, or any forms of communication, because they are universal symbols.

*****

In our journey in search of the golden bowls containing the quintile and sesquiquintile, we will use these tools: the numbers One through Five and the five geometric symbols, which are the vertical and horizontal lines, the circle, the triangle, and the square.

This amazing journey involves just those ten tools.

I can see how excited you are. Me, too! So grab your tool bag and we're off on our expedition.

CHAPTER 2

THE LEADER OF THIS EXPEDITION AND HIS TREASURE MAP

Around the sixth century BCE, Greece had Plato, Socrates, and Pythagoras, India had Buddha, and China had Confucius and Lao Tzu, the founder of Taoism.

Tao, pronounced "dah-o," means "the way." Tao is the universal principle that underlies everything. You might call Tao the Cosmic Egg.

After meeting Lao Tzu, Confucius told his students, "Birds can fly, Fish can swim, Animals can run, So they can all be snared or trapped. But Lao Tzu is like a flying Dragon, un-trappable."[1]

Did you notice that all these philosophers are men? Granted they were wise and all that but, come on, there had to have been a few intelligent gals out there somewhere around that time . . . just saying. I mean, the women were producing the babies, so they knew a little about creation!

But to give Lao Tzu his just due, he was a pretty smart guy; Confucius thought so. Lao Tzu wrote the most eloquent and concise truth about the creation of the cosmos that I have ever come across:

Tao generates One.

One generate Two.

Two generates Three.

Three generates 10,000 things.[2]

Some translators suggest that the last line reads: "Three generates all things." However, I expect Lao Tzu would have said "10,000 things"; you know, all those Zeros connected to the "One" implying infinity and the Cosmic Egg. He knew the power of the zero as an amplifier.

Lao Tzu's teaching sounds pretty simple, right? Almost like a grade school primer for children. But those simple lines are profound truths because they explain the fundamental creation process right down to the processes in our daily lives.

The truth is simple.

Intrigued yet? The steps will be so clear it will amaze you.

Let's begin with the Cosmic Egg. The ancient mystery schools explained number as the origin of all things. The Zero, technically not a number, (the Cosmic Egg, if you will), contains the numbers One through Nine, the progressive principles that emerge one from the other to create Life.

As stated, in this book we will concentrate on the five numbers One through Five, and the five geometric symbols, because they are the tools needed to uncover and prove the validity of the sacred aspects, the quintile and sesquiquintile. I encourage anyone interested in researching and studying this subject more thoroughly to refer to the suggested reading list at the back of this book.

Since it was universally accepted in ancient times that the Great Mother conceived the Universe in Her Cosmic Egg and gave birth to all that was, is, and would be, we can combine these two terms—Tao and Cosmic Egg—for perhaps a clearer picture of the sequential unfolding from the Zero.

Zero: the Tao, the Cosmic Egg, is that in which all things exist and happen—all that "is, was, and ever shall be."

> At some particular time in the past, then, all the matter and energy of the universe must have existed in one large lump . . . this zero-time can in fact be considered the beginning of our Universe."[3]

> It is misleading to describe the expansion of the universe as a sort of descending bubble viewed from the outside. By definition, nothing we can ever know about was outside.[4]

> Ten or twenty billion years ago, something happened . . . that began our universe . . . All the matter in the universe was concentrated at extremely high density—a kind of cosmic egg, reminiscent of the creation myths of many cultures—perhaps into a mathematical point with no dimensions at all.[5]

Zero is the "zero-time" when the universe was "one large lump," the Cosmic Egg.

Okay, I know you get the picture. I tend to repeat myself, the result of raising four children. So let's relate this process in more earthy terms. Life begins in the womb, that spherical shape from which life emerges. You might call the womb the Cosmic Egg waiting for the spark of creative energy. With the act of birth, we become co-creators with the Great Mother.

Back again to our expedition leader, Lao Tzu, the founder of Taoism and his simple truth:

> Tao generates One.
>
> One generate two.
>
> Two generates three.
>
> Three generates 10,000 things.

Tao is The Way, The Cosmic Womb

The Way is not to be seen as a route, as in "show me the way to San Jose." It's not the old television series *Route 66.*

Rather, The Way is a condition, a state of being. For instance, after trying to change a person to our liking, we might finally realize we cannot make that happen. So we give up in frustration because we realize "that's just the way she is, always has been, and always will be."

Tao is The Way, The Cosmic Womb, a state of being, unanimated.

Lao Tzu wrote: "Tao generates One"

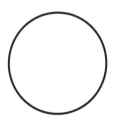

One is unity, symbolized by the circle because it is united and whole. It has no beginning and no end and is, therefore, eternal. As mentioned earlier, Voltaire wrote: "God is a circle whose center is everywhere and circumference is nowhere." I substitute "Mother" for "God"; Voltaire lived in a patriarchal world.

The "center is everywhere": Each of us is that center; we are each copies of the One. We should look within ourselves for our connection to the Mother. The "circumference is nowhere" implies we are limitless beings with untold potential.

These thoughts remind me of a favorite poem by Robert Frost, written in two simple elegant lines that speak truth.

We dance round in a ring and suppose,
But the Secret sits in the middle and knows.

Frost could have been describing the astrological chart. We chase our planets around the outer ring of the wheel, looking for love, job fulfillment, material possessions, and all that the physical world has to offer, when all along the Secret sits in the middle and knows. The Secret is you; you are in the center of the astrological wheel. When you truly know yourself, then you are fulfilled.

Lao Tzu wrote: "One generates Two."

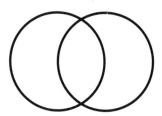

From the One, the Cosmic Egg, emerges the Two.

A circle emerging, birthing, from the One creates two equal and connected circles. Since we know that the ancients did not view Two as the addition of One and One but rather saw the Two as emerging from the One, we can relate this concept to the Mother giving birth to the Universe.

Carrying this concept further, the Earth mother gives birth to her child just as the female of any species gives birth or lays eggs. Birth was considered the closest act to divinity.

In the center of the two circles is the pointed oval called the Vesica Piscis (pronounced *vesica pis(k)s*), which in Latin means "bladder of a fish." This shape represents the genital area of the Great Mother, her vulva or vagina, the "divine opening or gateway," the holy sacred portal through which life emerges. Nicknames like "fish factories" have often been used to describe the female genital area.

The dictionary defines this almond shape created by the two intersecting circles as "an elliptical figure in pointed form, usually one made by the intersection of two arcs and used, especially in early Christian art, as an emblem of Christ...."

This is the doorway through which Christ was born. In religious and sacred literature in many cultures, the almond-shaped Vesica Piscis is often found surrounding sacred figures.

The "sacred figures" emerged from their mother's womb through her vagina, the vuvla, the Vesica Piscis, and out into life . . . just as we all do. The act of birth is sacred, the miracle of life.

The Pillars of the Temple, the Vesica Piscis, guard the doorway into the inner sanctum of the temple, the Cosmic Womb! These pillars can be seen on Key 2; The Priestess, in the Tarot deck. The Tarot has been called the book of life. Indeed, a story for another day.

This image of overlapping circles will figure importantly in the proof for the validity of the quintile and sesquiquintile.

In Two, opposites form. We begin to understand the relationships we must experience with the "other things" in our world in order to discover who we are. If we were alone in this world, we would not know ourselves because there is no "other," no mirror to reflect our actions back to us. Two implies awareness through opposites, the Yin and Yang.

Lao Tzu wrote: "Two generates Three."

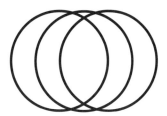

With the emergence of Three, time was born. The three is also symbolized by the joining of three straight lines in the form of the equilateral triangle.

The child, representative of the human race, was observed to go through three stages of growth in life: infancy, adulthood, and old age. This was more obvious with the female child: maiden, mother, crone.

In this three-stage process—past, present, and future, and birth, life, and death—time was recognized as the linear reality upon which the world of nature was built. Reflecting this reality, Three became the trinity in one form or another in all major religions.

Ancient religious icons often depict triple images of the Mother Goddess.

Lao Tzu wrote: "Three generates 10,000 things."

The Three-in-One concept behind trinities is the idea that within the One is the creative energy of the Three: Three generates life; Three generates 10,000 things.

Three generates everything in the Universe, which includes life here on Earth.

What do you think of this so far? Lao Tzu sure knew what he was talking about.

Time to shake the sand out of our shoes . . . we're moving on . . .

CHAPTER 3

UNCOVERING THE
THREE FROM THE SANDS
OF TIME

Three is Time.

As mentioned, Three is symbolized by the triangle, which has long been a religious symbol of the trinity. The Tantric Yoni Yantra, or downward pointing triangle, as is the symbol of the Primordial Mother, the source of all life. This triangle, a revered and adored symbol, represented the Mother's genital area from which all life emerged.

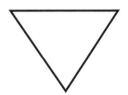 In Ancient societies, and in some contemporary ones, the triangle is recognized as the trinity of the Goddess in her three forms—Maiden, Mother, Crone.

The triangle was the Egyptian hieroglyphic symbol for woman. In the Greek alphabet, the symbol for delta is the triangle, signifying the Holy Door, vulva of the All-Mother-Demeter, Mother Delta.

The triangle symbolized a gathering of universal creative energy as can be seen in the Great Pyramid, which is considered to be a giant electrical conductor, an accumulator of creative energy awaiting release.

In 1859, Werner von Siemens, founder of the then-telecommunications company of the same name, climbed to the top of the Great Pyramid, with the help of Arab guides who "flung us on stage to stage like bales of goods."

At the top he heard a whistling noise, which he thought was the wind. The Arabs suddenly sprang up and cried "Chamsin" (which means "wretched wind") and held up their fore-fingers. Siemens did the same, and to his great surprise, he received a prickling sensation through his finger and also heard a sharp noise.

Curious by nature, he held up a full bottle of wine, the top covered with tinfoil. When he touched his other hand to the top of the wine bottle, he received a strong electric shock. It appeared to von Siemens that the Great Pyramid was an electrical conductor of some sort, a focus of creative energy.

Some historians believe that the Great Pyramid was not the tomb for a pharaoh but . . . an initiation temple. Here the candidate for initiation was laid on the granite sarcophagus for three-and-one-half days while the Ka, the candidate's soul, traveled the Universe gathering information and experience necessary for qualification as an adept. Some others believe the Great Pyramid is an energy source for extraterrestrial visitors.

The cone-shaped hats of witches and wizards are solidified triangles. Was this their way of drawing in the universal energy to enhance their feats of magic, of working with the natural forces of the Earth to bring about physical change?

In cartoons, the picture of a child on a stool wearing a dunce's cap evokes the feeling of a child who has not learned the lessons; the cone-shaped dunce hat perhaps signifying the need to energize the mind.

Places of religious worship often have steeples, exaggerated triangles, reaching high into the heavens as if to draw in the cosmic consciousness.

Our quest leader, Lao Tzu, spoke of the incredible energy of the triangle when he wrote: "Three generates 10,000 things."

A "thing" can only be defined when we compare one of the group of three to the other two. For instance, we can only know the present because of the past and the future; we only know space when we compare width to height and depth.

And from the Three:
All colors can be produced from red, yellow, and blue; music is composed of rhythm, tone, and harmony; a sound wave is amplitude, frequency, and phase. And there is Sir Isaac Newton's three laws of motion. "Nearly all subsequent mechanics have been based upon his conclusions, and it is really astonishing to note how often the most recondite analyses in this field turn out to be only reaffirmations of his principles."[1]

The above reasons may be why the ancient Chinese considered the number One to have the same value as the Three. It seems the ancient Egyptians held this belief as well. The idea of divinity as Three-in-One, or the triangle within the circle, takes on new meaning when viewed in this light.

See how amazing the tools of geometry are, how they can dig up truths through symbols?

We can now understand why we say "things happen in threes." We don't say "things happen in twos" or "things happen in 8s," and that's because we subconsciously understand the meanings of the metaphysical principles of numbers and basic geometric symbols, those principles that remain constant and unchanging. They are truths through which our common expressions emerge.

The Riddle of the Sphinx embodies this trinitarian principle of time. When the prince Oedipus approached the city of Thebes, he found the road blocked by a monster called the Sphinx who had the body of a lion and the head of a woman. Only those who answered the riddle correctly could pass; those who answered incorrectly were killed.

The Sphinx asked: what walked on four feet in the morning, two feet at noon, and three feet in the evening. No one had answered correctly until Oedipus. He answered that it was the human who crawls during infancy, walks upright on two feet during adult years, and uses a cane in old age. He got a pass.

You've heard the expression "as wise as Solomon." This common expression has a connection to time and knowledge.

From three ancient languages: in Latin, *sol* means "sun"; in Hindu Sanskrit *om* or *aum* means "sun"; and in Egyptian, *on* means "sun." *Sol* is the rising Sun in the East; *om* or *aum* is the sun at it highest point; and *on* is the setting sun in the West.

The name *Sol-Om-On*, in its three phases, traces the Sun's journey each day, the period of daylight, when we can see.

Solomon embodies the concept that with the passage of time . . . each day that passes from sunrise to noon to sunset . . . we become wiser through the experiences we encounter living life. By experiencing each day in the light, we become Solomons, those who see the Light!

Light is a symbol of awareness shown through another common expression: I see the light.

Solomon was an office, like the Presidency, that was bestowed on the wise. There were a number of Solomons in history such a Salmanu from Babylonia. The Solomons of Babylonia presided over the temples dedicated to "divine wisdom," or we might say these temples were dedicated to divine Light, or knowledge.

The Tower of Babel was one such edifice.

The Christian story of Babel in Genesis states that, after the Great Flood, the Great Cleansing, everyone on earth spoke the same language. The people migrated from the east and built a great tower tall enough to reach heaven. God saw this as disrespectful, therefore, he confounded their speech so they could no longer understand each other.

This parable explains how speaking the same language, understanding the wisdom of living in the Light, and migrating from the East, where the Sun rises each day to shed the Light, creates a society where people live in harmony and truth.

When these people built the Tower of Babel, they were creating the false narratives of civilization, where the Light had been lost beneath human desires and arrogance, and that's when the people became confused.

I do get carried away with the Three. But, as you can see, there is so much embedded in this simple number and its symbolic expression, the triangle. There is more, but I'm sure at this point, I've said enough.

Just remember that all this information came from the Three, which emerged from the Two, which emerged from the One, and is symbolized by the equilateral triangle. You can see how the numbers and geometry have such vast stories to tell.

Yes, thanks to Lao Tzu, we now know that, "Three generates 10,000 things."

So, let's trek on.

CHAPTER 4

UNCOVERING
THE FOUR FROM THE
SANDS OF TIME

I'll bet you never thought we'd get to the Four, but here we are.

Lao Tzu's description stops at the Three, because, as he wrote: "Three generates 10,000 things." However, in the natural progression of numbers, it is out of the Three-in-One principle that the Four emerges.

Four is the square, the second perfect shape that can be constructed with straight lines.

 The square is a symbol of form. Its extension, the cube, is the symbol for the physical body and the material world. Remember the illustration earlier where the Christian cross can be folded into a cube.

However, the Four has been given a bad rap!

For two millennia, the Judeo-Christian tradition has taught that the physical must be denied to attain the spiritual. The Western philosophy of denying the pleasures of the physical for some greater reward in a celestial realm where everything is wonderful and pure and full of light, devoid of the sensual desires of life itself, is reflected in what some more modern numerologists have written about the Four: Four is a drudge and a burden and can only be endured; Four does not easily find happiness and joy; Four is dull, uninteresting, and uninspired; and so forth.

This attitude of denying the physical plane for the spiritual plane does reflect this Age of Pisces that we have been experiencing for the last 2,000 years. However, the Piscean Age is ending: We are on the brink of the Age of Aquarius. Big changes are occurring.

It's important to remember that whatever you read comes from the mind of the writer; it is her personal background that creeps into the narrative. It is almost impossible to separate who we are from what we write. And that includes me. So, always accept information at face value, then process it, see what works for you, and discard the rest. Or maybe just tuck it into one of those wrinkles in your brain for future reference. Who knows, you might want to pull it out at some time in the future.

Negative comments about the number Four deny the Spirit in Matter. They deny the spiritual processes of nature with the magical play of light over the equator that creates the seasons. They deny the existence of the soul of the Earth. These deniers seek to separate us from nature outside of ourselves as well as from our inborn natures that seek pleasure in good food, the feel of slipping into something silky, the caressing touch of a hand, the blending of bodies in intimate embrace. In this denial process we have become spiritual paupers.

In a PBS series hosted by Bill Moyers called *The Power of Myth*, Joseph Campbell told the story of an Asian sage speaking to a group of Westerners about their belief system. "God against man, man against God, man against nature, nature against man, nature against God. Very funny religion."[1]

As a result, the number Four, the number of Mother Earth, and its corporeal pleasures that have been connected with the female, has come down to us as something "spiritual" people should avoid and shun. Those normal feelings have been stuffed into our unlit closets. No wonder Freud had such a heyday with the frustrated sexual energies of his Victorian period, as well as his own.

If a numerologist tells you that the number Four is grossly material, dull and uninspired, a drudge and a complainer, ask them how they feel about sex and food, an eagle on the wind, and daffodils in the spring, snowflakes on the window pane, and the birth of a child.

The Four is also connected to the Earth through the four seasons of the year. Symbolically forming a cross, the equinoxes and solstices mark the "crossing points," the end of the old, and the beginning of the new, the Earth's eternal cycle of quarterly rebirths.

This crossing also designates points of reference in our calendars that provide information about the kind of weather we can expect in our region, the cycles of planting, even the phases of sales in the market place. This four-point division provides earth-related information.

In astrology, the sensitive angles of the chart—the Ascendant, Descendant, MC, and IC—represent the cross, which gives information about the four basic divisions of our individual earthly lives: the self, the other, the home, and the world.

Two planets separated by 90 degrees sit each on two adjacent arms of a cross. This is called a "square" and is a revealing and powerful aspect. The square is the energized portion of the chart because it creates a stress point that lets you know in no uncertain terms that you are alive. The square is a point that has to be recognized and dealt with or it will continue to unsettle you throughout your life.

In the astrological square, there is a need to find that point of consciousness, where the two challenging forces intersect, so that you can learn from that stress and allow that knowledge to become a substantial building block supporting your life. Often, once this square is recognized and overcome, it becomes your strongest attribute.

The first two so-called perfect forms in geometry are the triangle and the square because they are the first two visible shapes that can be constructed with straight lines.

Once again, the square, the Four, symbolizes the world of Matter, the physical realm in which we live.

In 1916, thirty-third-degree mason Frank C. Higgins, wrote in his book *Hermetic Masonry* that some of the most important features of God's creation are "inextricably built around the precise geometrical relation of a square and a circle . . ."[2]

Because so much of the esoteric side of the ritual in masonry was lost to the general Masonic member of his time, he went on to say that ". . . masonry has become a pale shadow of the old world craft."

To the learned ones of the past, nature or matter was the container of the Life Force. Matter contained the Light; Matter was Spirit made manifest.

You might say Matter is solidified Light! Which brings to mind . . .

One day, while riding in the car with my husband for a number of miles in silence, he suddenly said, "You know, we're just temporary manifestations of light."

I blinked, and turned toward this plaid-clad man, my frontier woodsman husband, and exclaimed, "Where did that come from?"

He just shrugged and said, "I don't know. I was just thinking."

There is something to be said about communing with nature . . . the flora and the fauna . . . the squirrels and the deer, the mountain trails, camping, and canoeing. What a guy!

Anyway . . . for our ancestors, there was no distinction or separation between Nature and Spirit while in the physical body. This ancient belief parallels today's scientific discovery that our physical bodies are composed of the debris of stars that exploded millions of years ago; we are literally star children or solidified Light.

Recently, an astronomer noted: The Bible says from dust to dust; we say from stardust to stardust. We are made of the stars.

I've always been flummoxed by mathematical equations. They are a different language than the language of geometry we are using in this book, so I have to work slowly through the formulas that follow here.

As mentioned above, in the natural progression of numbers, Three generates the Four symbolized by the square: Four is the ruler of the physical world of form.

Four is the only one of the nine numbers that determines equal value in both the area and circumference of a circle and equal value in both the area and circumference of a square. In other words, symbolically, Four is the only value that determines form.

Definitions:

A=Area, the amount of space inside the boundary of a flat space.

C=Circumference, the distance around the outside edge of a shape.

D=Diameter, the straight passing from side to side through the exact center of a shape

R=Radius, half the diameter.

Π=Pi, a mathematical constant representing the ratio of the circumference of a circle to its diameter.

Following is the mathematical reason why the number Four is the only value that determines equal value in both the area and circumference of a circle and square.

The square:

The formula for the circumference of a square: add the four sides.

If each of those four sides measures 4 inches, then the circumference, the distance around the outside, totals 16 inches. (4+4+4+4=16)

The formula for the area of the square: multiply one side by one side.

Using the 4: 4x4=16. In this case, the area is also 16. (4x4=16)

Four determines equal value both in the area and circumference of a square.

This is not true using the other single numbers 1, 2, 3, 5, 6, 7, 8, and 9.

The circle:

The formula for the circumference of a circle is C=Πd.

Using the number 4 as the diameter, the formula reads: C=Π4.www

The formula for the area of the circle is A=Πr².

Using the number four, the formula reads:
A=Π x the radius (which is 2) squared, or A=Π x (2x2) or A=Π4.

The 4 determines equal value in the circumference and surface of a circle.

I just barely made it through that tangled web, which proves mathematically that Four is the only number that determines equal value in both the area and circumference of a circle and a square.

Remember, in the language of geometry, the circle is Spirit and the square is Matter. The ancients saw number as the philosophical reduction of principles, so this uniqueness of the Four indicated that Spirit (the circle) and Matter (the square) were one in the same because they had equal value.

In mythological literature, the flora and fauna of the garden (the square, the earth) connected the worshipper to the elevated being (Spirit) that personified one's religion; in some cultures, there were many Spirits. These gardens were always described as "blissful," a place where one was closest to the Creator.

In Christianity, there is the Garden of Eden; in Greek mythology, the Garden of the Hesperides; the Japanese word for garden, *niwa*, means a place that had been purified in anticipation of the deified spirits of Shinto; the word "rosary" means rose garden.

Funny. I just noticed for the first time after all these years of sitting in front of the keyboard that the dollar sign is on the same key as the number 4. Four relates to the material world, which in most societies, includes money as a medium of exchange. In more "primitive" societies, your wealth could be measured in pigs and cows.

No one seems to know where the symbol for the dollar sign originated, although there is much speculation. Some believe the symbol "$" represents the snake wound around the tree in the Garden of Eden, or the snakes wound around the staff of the Caduceus, both of which relate to Spirit in Matter.

In Matter, in the material world, money is used as a medium of exchange to purchase material goods; it is used to build great cities of culture or to wage wars of total destruction. Money is neither good nor bad; it's what we do to get it and what we do with it that counts.

I wonder who set up the keyboard and if they knew . . . We should always ask questions, because that's how we learn.

Anyway, you're in luck because you're out there, and I'm in here, and I can't ask you any questions. But I do hope you have a lot of your own questions that will continue to intrigue you. It's important to exercise our little gray cells.

Yes, the Four. The Four has obvious associations with the Earth in terms like "the four corners of the earth," even though the Earth is more spherical. We have the four winds, the four compass points, the four seasons. And then there's the common expression, a "square meal," which is a meal that nourishes the body.

The big Four is the four fundamental forces in nature: electromagnetism, gravity, and the strong and weak nuclear forces. These are the four fundamental glues that keep our material world functioning.

So, Three generates Four, the world of nature in its form.

The chart I composed, shown here, lists a number of well-known divisions of Four related to the material world, categorized under the classic four elements: Fire, Water, Air, and Earth.

In the Judaic Old Testament, there are numerous names for "God," depending upon the meaning involved. The four-part name of God, called the Tetragrammaton, is Jod-Heh-Vau-Heh, or Jehovah. Note the four part name of God in this chart.

THE FOUR ELEMENTS
THE BUILDING BLOCKS OF LIFE
Their Expression in the Physical World

Elements	Fire	Water	Air	Earth
Seasons	Spring	Summer	Fall	Winter
Tarot Suits	Wands	Cups	Swords	Pentacles
Playing Card Suits	Clubs	Hearts	Spades	Diamonds
Tetragammatron	Jod	Heh	Vau	Heh
Sacred Trapezoid	10	5	6	5
Serpent Signs	Leo	Scorpio	Aquarius	Taurus
Astrological Types	Ardent	Emotional	Intellectual	Practical
Apostles	Mark	John	Matthew	Luke
World Myth Figures (i.e., Sphinx)	Lion	Eagle	Woman	Bull
Nature Spirits (Paracelsus)	Salamander	Undines	Sylphs	Gnomes
Greek Philosophical Qualities	Morality	Aesthetics	Intellectuality	Physicality
Human	Spirit	Soul	Mind	Body
Human Functions (Jung)	Intuition	Feeling	Thinking	Sensation
Human Bodies	Vital/ Etheric	Emotional/ Astral	Mental/ Casual	Physical

Through Gematria, once again applying number values to letters of the Hebrew alphabet, the numbers of Jod-Heh-Vau-Heh are 10-5-6-5. These are the values used to construct the Sacred Trapezoid as a geometrical symbol of Jehovah. A trapezoid, in this case, is a flat diagram with two parallel sides and two slanted legs. See the diagram below.

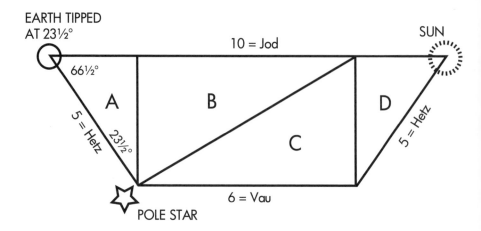

This Sacred Trapezoid depicts the physical position of the Earth in relation to the Sun! This illustration shows the Earth's fixed polar tip at a 23½-degree angle towards the Sun on its yearly journey around our star. Without this polar tip toward the Sun, we would not experience the movement of light over the equator, which creates the four seasons. Without the four seasons, we would not have life on this planet as we now experience it.

The different names of "God" indicate the specific process in effect when that specific name is used. Jehovah is the god that creates the seasons, that creates the environment in which we live. The seasons provide the opportunity for us to live our lives and gain the wisdom of our years lived. The Old Testament's Jehovah or Jod-Heh-Vau-Heh, is God operating through the physical world.

The undulating motion of the Sun's light up and down over the equator every year is personified in symbols such as the snake, the serpent, and the dragon. These creatures represent wisdom, because it is within this undulating passage of the seasons, as the days and months go by, that we have the opportunity to grow and become wise.

Years ago I read a wonderful beginner's book on astrology by Ove Sehested (*The Basics of Astrology,* the second in his three-set series) in which he presented a visual example of the Earth's journey around the Sun.

I love visuals. They remind me of the Golden Book Encyclopedia that I carried around as a child, an oversized hardcover book full of colored illustrations and the meanings of words! What a treasure!

Anyway, Ove Sehested suggested taking the shade off a lamp, turning it on, and placing the lamp in a position where you can safely walk around it. Then, using a Styrofoam[R] ball, poke a long knitting needle or some such object through the exact middle of the ball. The needle represents the north and south poles of the Earth. Then draw a dark line around the middle of the ball approximately where the equator would be.

In a darkened room, with the ball constantly tipped toward the lamp at what you would estimate is about a 23° angle, walk completely around the lamp. Watch how the light from the lamp moves up and down over the dark line, which is the equator on the ball. You will see that the light from the lamp goes up a short distance over the equator and then begins to move down over the equator as you walk around the lamp. This snake-like movement over the ball represents the seasons on our planet.

See the illustration shown here.
Jehovah is the name of the Hebrew "God" that was directly connected to the physical world with its four seasons, which connects to the number Four. This is the Jehovah of the Old Testament that was written in Hebrew.

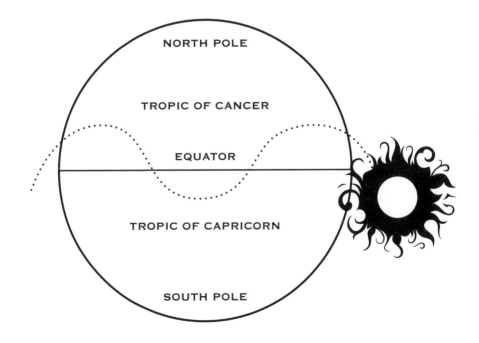

These are the treasures we discover when we know how to use the tools of numbers and geometry.

The following quote by our Masonic friend, Frank C. Higgins, from his 1923 book *Ancient Freemasonry*, is the crux of the language of numbers:

Almost all the ancient names of Deity, when their letters are resolved into numbers, are found to consist of what are sometimes called "cosmic numbers" in that they express some great planetary or terrestrial cycles.

As mentioned, there were other ancient names for the Creator depending upon the activity involved. Jehovah is one of the most recognizable names in the Western world today, and it is one of the names of deity that is directly related to the physical world and everyday life on the physical plane, this place where we live within the rhythm of the four seasons that regulate our planet.

I know—I'm repeating myself. But you have to admit this is pretty illuminating.

The Four is Spirit in Matter; nature is spiritual.

When I first came across this information, I needed time to absorb it. Maybe you want to "take time to think today."

Actually, this line comes from a book entitled *Handwriting Analysis* by M. N. Bunker. No relation. He claims that your handwriting shows who you are and, if you changed your handwriting, you could change your life.

He suggested to a suicidal friend that if he wrote the line "take time to think today" forty times each night for forty nights and crossed the "t's" high up the stem and pressed heavily on the paper and then underlined his signature three times, it would change his life.

And it did.

Crossing the "t's" high up the stem lifted his consciousness to a higher level (the vertical line symbol); these two lines form the crossing point of Spirit into Matter. Pressing heavily under his name (the horizontal line symbol) indicated the intensity of his determination in this physical world.

And the forty times represents the number Four, the physical body, the Earth, and in this case, the cross he bore.

You see how ubiquitous symbols are. They can change your life!

CHAPTER 5

UNCOVERING THE FIVE FROM THE SANDS OF TIME

Five is the quickening, the number of life itself.

The "quickening" takes place within the form. Form itself is not "alive" in the sense we know it—a body has form but no life—until the quickening takes place. In a pregnancy we speak of the fifth month as the quickening, that time when the mother first feels the baby move.

In early cultures it was generally accepted that the soul did not enter the fetus until the fifth month of pregnancy, therefore, the fetus could be aborted prior to this time without punishment. Prior to 1869, the Catholic Church's Doctrine of Passive Conception concurred with this belief, and abortion prior to the fifth month was not considered a crime. Before the fifth month, the fetus was the form, the Four, without the life breath; the soul entered that form through the animating Five.

There is an "old wife's tale" (the old wife is the Crone in Mother Goddess religion who is revered for her wisdom) that says illnesses turn for better or worse in the fifth hour, the fifth day, the fifth week, the fifth year.

Five has always been recognized as the pivotal point in cycles when a change in the physical will occur. Of course, the most elementary change in the physical is when the soul enters or leaves the body.

Five is called the keystone in the arch of life because it is the central number in the cosmic blueprint represented by the natural order of the numbers One through Nine.

With the quickening, the Four is animated by the Five, symbolic of Life.

Ancient philosophers and alchemists used the five-pointed star, the Pentagram, to symbolize the human being as a miniature replica of the greater life pattern of the cosmos. The pentagram has been called the pentacle, the pentangle, the pentalpha, the Devil's sign, the Witches' Cross and Witches' Foot, the Wizard's Star, the Goblin's Cross, the Star of Knowledge, and the Pentacle of the Virgin. Quite a variety of names evoking a variety of responses, both positive and negative.

Some people today still react to the five-pointed star as something evil . . . the Devil's Sign. This comes from the early church's need to keep the people's sensual needs under control, because Five represents the five senses with which the human is endowed and which the church felt they should deny. This may be why the priests and nuns did not marry; they were denying the life-affirming experiences of the physical world by vowing allegiance to the spiritual world.

The full use of the senses allows people the ability to experience life to its fullest, which would include sensual pleasure, the accumulation of knowledge, and independent thinking.

THE PENTAGRAM

Our friend, German astronomer Kepler, introduced the fifth division of the circle. See the illustration above. The tips of the star touch the circumference of the circle dividing it into divisions of 72°, the quintile aspect, one of our golden bowls, which is said to be "mildly beneficial." We will soon know better.

Our five senses are highlighted under this number shown by the example of the apple chosen by many cultures as the epitome of knowledge. Petrified slices of apples on plates have been found in tombs dating back 5,000 years.

If you slice an apple horizontally, you will find five seeds in the shape of a pentagram. It was when Adam ate the apple that Eve picked for him that they both took on conscious awareness through their five senses.

Yet, the story goes that while Eve busted her buns picking Adam an apple, he eats it, and then she gets blamed for the sin of their having to leave their comfy home in the Garden of Eden. That's the way the patriarchs have told the story these past few thousand years.

The point here is that eating the apple gave Adam and Eve the opportunity to leave the garden (the Four) and move out in the world of sensual experience and knowledge (the Five).

The Druids had seven sacred trees, one of which was the apple tree. They considered apples the fruit of the gods.

In Greek mythology, the daughters of the night, the four Hesperides, guarded the golden apples that grew in a sumptuous garden at the edge of the world.

The Four daughters of the night and the Garden: Four represents the physical form, night implies not being able to see the light, and the Garden is the container, the Four, not yet animated.

Eating the golden apples, symbolic of the Five, animates the five senses, bestowing the opportunity to experience life and gain knowledge. The animation brings the light of knowledge; Light represents knowledge.

In the stories of the Garden of Eden and the Garden of the Hesperides, change occurred (the animating spark of life, the Five) when one left the confined spaces (the gardens, the Four).

When you know the meaning behind the numbers and the geometric shapes, a whole new world opens. This is the language of sacred numbers and sacred geometry that tell the complete story that is hidden behind parables and myths.

Five is the number of change because it represents nature or Life, which is in a constant state of flux. One of the laws of physics is that the only constant is change. This is the law of five, the Law of Life.

Perhaps you might want to read these past chapters more than once. I certainly have! We learn through repetition.

Okay, time for a breather. Pull out those dark chocolate peanut clusters and plop down on the recliner where you can veg out and satisfy your body while you feed your mind. And then we'll trek on to the next chapter which uncovers the Divine Triangle.

CHAPTER 6

UNCOVERING THE PYTHAGOREAN THEOREM FROM THE SANDS OF HIGH SCHOOL MATH CLASS

The discovery of this mathematical formula, the Pythagorean Theorem, was monumental. This formula was and still is used in the laying out of structures. The Pythagorean formula is essential in order to place the corner stones of a building squarely. The strength and final successful outcome of that structure depends upon this mathematical accuracy. Tipsy churches and buildings were not built to last.

The "laying of the cornerstone" is spoken of in symbolic terms in metaphysical literature. Think: the temple not built with human hands (which is the human body).

So, let's talk about the classic 3-4-5 right triangle that many of us struggled with in high school math class. Named after the Greek philosopher Pythagoras, the Pythagorean Theorem states that the square of the hypotenuse (the slanted line) is equal to the sum of the squares of the other two sides. This following equation is straightforward. When you square a number, you multiply it by itself. Using the classic 3-4-5 right triangle shown here:

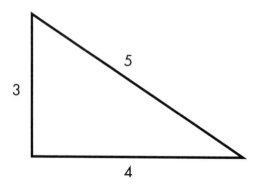

First we square each of the three sides:

- the 3 side squared (3x3) equals 9
- the 4 side squared (4x4) equals 16.
- the hypotenuse squared (5x5) equals 25

So, the sum of the squares of the two sides (9+16) equals the square of the hypotenuse (25).

Behind the use of this mathematical formula is the spiritual formula that brought about the creation of the Universe.

The Pythagorean Theorem, which constructs what is called the Divine Triangle, is a universal truth that states that the sum of Three (Time) plus the sum of Four (Space) results in the sum of Five (Life).

Time and Space create Life.

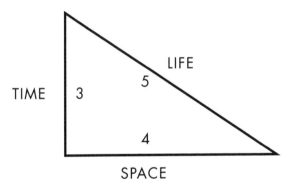

This is the hidden truth that is described in Lao Tzu's teaching about the orderly creation of the Universe: Three generates 10,000 things.

We attribute this theorem to Pythagoras (circa 580 BCE), the Greek philosopher, mathematician, and teacher mentioned above, who brought it to our attention. But it was well known long before his time.

A Chinese astronomical and mathematical treatise called Chou Pei Suan Ching, possibly predating Pythagoras, gives a geometrical demonstration of the "Pythagorean" theorem. And ancient Indian mathematicians (800–600 BCE) also knew of the right triangle formula.

A clay token (tessera) from about 2,000 BCE, upon which this 3-4-5 triangle was inscribed, was found in an Egyptian tomb.

Ancient clay tablets from Babylonia (2,000 BCE) understood the relationships amongst the three sides of the right triangle and were able to solve the mathematics of their construction projects using this formula.

This right triangle formula was the basic blueprint for the construction of ancient buildings and temples but, as the Divine Triangle, it is the cosmic blueprint for the construction of the human temple, the body, and life itself.

The Divine Triangle has been and is today the foundation of the world's major religions.

As above; so below.

To refresh your memory about the meaning of these numbers, you might want to go back and reread the chapters on the Three, which represents Time; the Four, which represents the physical world; and the Five, which is the quickening of Life within the physical world.

CHAPTER 7

UNCOVERING THE QUINTILE AND SESQUIQUINTILE FROM THE SANDS OF TIME

The Cosmic Trinity—Three-Four-Five—is called the Divine Triangle. This was the ultimate secret taught at all the ancient mystery schools. And this is the hidden truth that has emerged from Lao Tzu's teaching about the orderly creation of the Universe. The Divine Triangle is the cosmic blueprint for creation.

As mentioned in the last chapter, the right triangle formula was used to lay the cornerstone in the building of ancient churches and temples, and is used today for the construction of modern buildings.

It is also upon this sacred triangle that the world religions are based! The "gods" worshiped throughout the world's religions were birthed from this triangle that emerged from the Mother's Cosmic Egg.

Iconic images like the Vesica Piscis surrounding holy figures and the triple figures of goddesses are the external wrapping, which cloth the hidden message of creation in human terms. Religions give names to their gods who express the life-giving Three through the three members of their trinities.

We find holy trinities throughout cultures: Osiris-Isis-Horus; Brahma-Vishnu-Shiva; Buddha is defined by three bodies of enlightenment; and we have the Christian Father-Son-Holy Ghost. The Holy Ghost is the Mother. The early church patriarchs tried to eliminate the feminine aspect, but the people would not give up the Mother image; the compromise was Mary, the Holy Virgin, who exists outside the trinity.

Religion reflects the consciousness of a people. We experience Time, we understand Space, and we contain the animating force of Life. This process is built into our psyches, therefore, we create parables, myths, and human families to play out what we innately know as truth. We translate and humanize the Divine Triangle into something we can relate to on earthly terms!

These are the external voices that reflect the subliminal truth of creation.

Once again, apply the language of geometry and numbers to the creation message and see the hidden truth:

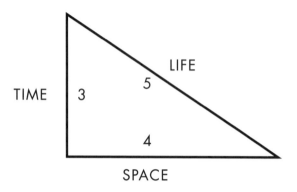

As we followed Lao Tzu, we have learned:

In the Beginning was the Cosmic Egg, the Tao:

Tao generates One:

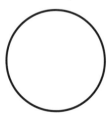

One generate Two:

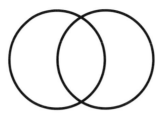

Two generates Three:

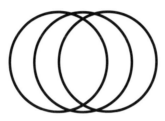

Three generates 10,000 things.
Now, let's place the Divine Triangle inside a circle.

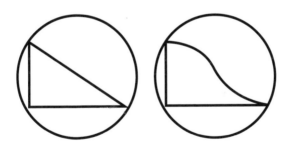

In the illustration above showing the Divine Triangle inside the circle, you can almost visualize an eye. The illustration on the right is the All-Seeing Eye depicted in Egyptian hieroglyphs.

Called the Eye of Horus, it was originally personified in the Goddess Wadjet whose name means "the green one." She was the Cobra Goddess, the protector of Lower Egypt who supposedly took the title of the Eye of Ra, so says history (his-story). Ra is the male personification of the life-giving force, the Sun.

I say give credit where it's due. I believe, given the proof presented in this book, the correct name for the Eye of Horus should be the Eye of Wadjet. As the Cobra Goddess, she was the Life Force.

As discussed earlier, undulating creatures like the snake depicted the Sun's movement over the Earth, which created the seasons in which we live, basically creating Life on our green planet. Snakes represent wisdom gained through living life.

One of the Egyptian hieroglyphs for the eye means "to make or to do." Wadjet was the Cosmic Mother who made the Universe.

Ancient Egyptians and Middle Eastern sailors often painted the Eye of Wadjet on the bows of their vessels to ensure their safety. They wanted the protection of the Mother energy.

The Eye of Wadjet is also depicted on the back of the American one dollar bill. Her Eye is enclosed in a triangle separated from the top of a pyramid where she watches over the pyramid, life's electrical conductor, to keep tabs on what we're doing.

Now you know why you sometimes feel like someone is either watching you or watching over you. Depends upon whether you're naughty or nice. I sure don't want to mess with her.

Now, the Egyptians, understanding this sacred process of the One-Two-Three, which produced Time, Space, and Life, placed the Divine Triangle, with its measurements of 3-4-5, within the three circles that emerged from the Cosmic Egg. See the diagram below.

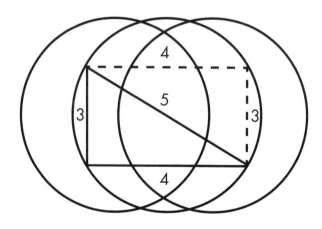

Our diagram is beginning to look complicated, but now it should be clear how we arrived at this point and what the sacred geometry before us indicates.

To simplify this illustration, let's place the Divine Triangle inside the center of one circle, the One, and extend lines of the triangle to form a rectangle.

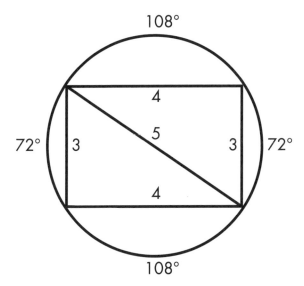

Look closely. The opposing arcs of the circle measure 72° and 108°!

And there they are! The arcs outside the rectangle are the Golden Bowls of the Egyptians!

I call this the Golden Bowl Rectangle!

We have uncovered the hidden treasure . . . the sacred golden bowls of the Egyptians, the quintiles and the sesquiquintiles, the Pillars of the Temple, the most creative of all the aspects in astrology!

Let's raise our bubbly in a toast for our expedition leader, Lao Tzu. He had it right all along.

After our long journey, our celebration for finding the treasure, and the recuperation period from all that champagne, we are surely exhausted, so let's take a few days to recuperate.

And take note that, in Hermetic Masonry, Frank C. Higgins wrote: "The Egyptians, circumscribing the oblong of 3 x 4 with a perfect circle, found the latter divided into segments of 72, 108, 72, 108 degrees. Such saucer-shaped segments were among their most sacred symbols . . ."[1]

I have named this pattern the Golden Bowl Rectangle: two quintiles connected by two sesquiquintiles.

Just think! You have learned two new languages. And it only took five numbers and five symbols! How amazing is that!

I don't know about you but I'm ready for a long winter's nap while the Eye of Wadjet watches over me.

CHAPTER 8

THE COSMIC EGG AND MONET

On our early morning walk down a local country road, my husband and I passed a sign at the end of a dirt drive that read: FRESH EGGS—$3.00 A DOZEN.

A short while later, we stopped by a gently rippling river where I performed my brief morning ritual with the words: "I welcome the bounty of the earth and the bounty of the heaven." After a few deep breaths of the misty air, we turned and headed back to the point where we passed the same sign.

My mind had been wrapped around the Cosmic Egg for the last six months. So, each time I passed that sign, I was reminded of this manuscript.

So, it was natural for me to wonder if Mama Hen and Cosmic Mother have something in common. My friend and fellow astrologer Mike Levesque, designed and found the formula that connects the egg shown here to the golden bowls of the Egyptians, the 72 and 108 degree aspects.

THE DIVINE CREATIVITY RATIO EGG

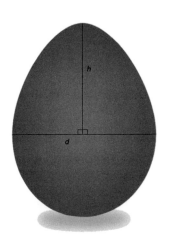

d = the diameter at its greatest circular girth

h = the height from the center of the circle to the apex

The diameter and the height are in a 1.333... (3 infinitely repeats) ratio denoted as "k" the constant in the equation: $d / k = h$.

For example: If the diameter of 144 units is known, then 144 (d) divided by 1.333... (k) equals 108 (h) expressed as: 144 units / 1.333 . . . = 108 units.

Note: The 144, which is two quintiles, and the 108, which is the sesquiquintile.

CLAUDE MONET (1840–1926)
BRIDGE AT BOUVIGAL

Monet sectioned off his canvas from the four edges using the golden ratio to produce the vertical and horizontal golden ratio lines shown here. By placing specific subject matter relative to these divisions arranged by foreground, middle ground, and background zones, he created a landscape most aesthetically pleasing to the eye.

A small sampling: the lower golden ratio line runs through the woman holding the child's hand placing them in the key foreground position as well as creating a transition zone from the river bank edge to the village leading the viewer's eye from left to right settling back again in the middle. The upper line separates the middle ground of the land and village from the sky.

The far left vertical line marks the transition zone between the bridge and the river. This same line emphasizes the vertical trees lining the bridge. The right vertical line draws the eye along the road that leads to the village and sky.

The Golden Ratio is the secret formula behind the Creator's mathematical precision in creating the Universe right down to the face of the sunflower.

Credit once again goes to Mike Levesque for his research, selection, and the information provided here for the analysis of this painting as representative of the golden ratio.

CHAPTER 9

THE POT OF GOLD

I just can't help myself. Here are a few more jewels hidden beneath the numbers. Certainly if you are still hanging in here with me at this point, you will want to dip your hands into this pot and watch the gems and gold nuggets tumble through your fingers.

So, why not settle down with your box of dark chocolate peanut clusters—I assume you still have some left—and let's do a bit more exploring.

THE FIBONACCI SEQUENCE
AND THE GOLDEN RATIO

Let's talk about the Fibonacci sequence. This is a series of numbers that start with either 0 and 1, or 1 and 1. The first two numbers are added, and then in the sequence that follows, each succeeding number is the result of the addition of the previous two.

For instance, starting with 0 and 1, the series runs 0, 1, 1, 2, 3, 5, 8, 13, 21, 34, 55, 89, 144, and so on. Named after the twelfth-century Italian mathematician Leonardo Fibonacci, the sequence had been described earlier by Indian mathematicians. This series exhibits a pattern found in art and nature, science and mathematics, and in the spiral of our Milky Way galaxy.

Much of nature grows in a heliacal pattern using the Fibonacci numbers.

Around its central core, a daisy has tiny florets in opposing spirals, usually 21 going left and 34 spiraling right. The mountain aster often has 13 spirals going left and 21 to the right. And in its spectacular glory, the sunflower has 55 spirals in one direction and 89 in the other. These are all Fibonacci numbers.

The ratio between successive Fibonacci numbers reveals a mathematical constant called the "golden mean" or phi (Φ), the value of which is approximately 1.618. When the golden mean ratio is applied to nature and art in any form, to buildings and to the proportions of the human body and face, we see the hand of beauty at work.

The Greeks used the golden ratio in the construction of their temples because they knew that these proportions were the most aesthetically pleasing. The Parthenon is a perfect example. The Great Pyramid contains ratios equal to the golden ratio, and so do the works of Da Vinci. Virgil, Beethoven, and Mozart are said to have employed this ratio.

To arrive at the golden ratio, use a line 8 inches long and divide it into two segments, one 5 inches, the other 3 inches (Fibonacci numbers).

Divide the longer line (5) by the shorter line (3).

$$5/3 = 1.666$$

Now, divide the total length of the line (8) by the longer line (5).

$$8/5 = 1.6$$

The result is 1.6, which approximates the golden mean of 1.618.

Through the use of these proportions beauty emerges.

As stated, nature exhibits her beauty in this Golden ratio. The wise builders knew this divine proportion and used this ratio in the building of the ancient temples, which are still considered beautiful to this day. And the Golden ratio is the proportion we find aesthetically pleasing in the human body and face.

The Ages and the 144,000 saved:

In Revelations in the Christian Bible, the writer speaks of the 144,000 saved, or the number of "spiritual" souls who will be saved at the "end of the world." 144 is one of the Fibonacci numbers.

The word "world" could also be read as "age." So, this passage could be interpreted as the number of souls who will be saved at the end of the Age, for instance this Age of Pisces. Most likely the "end of the world" refers to the Precession of the Equinoxes. An age is said to last about 2,160 years.

Remember that in sacred geometry and numbers, the use of zeros after numbers was an emphasis or empowering of the numbers involved. The doubling of numbers represents the energy magnified.

The sum of the two golden bowls of 72° equals 144°. These are the souls who are saved by drinking from the golden bowls of creation. So, if you're really good and fulfill your destiny, you will be deemed worthy of saving. But that's a patriarchal look at the process; the Great Mother welcomes all back into her fold.

The pair of 72° arcs (which total 144) are the "Pillars of the Temple," the Vesica Piscis, of which we have spoken at length. These are the gateways to a new life, the portals through which we pass into this life through the Cosmic Mothers genital area.

The 144,000 saved is all of us, all of humanity. We are all the saved through the sacred process of birth, death, and rebirth from the womb of creation through the Vesica Pisics, which are the 72° Pillars of the Temple.

Through these temple portals, we move on to the next life where, as new temporary manifestations of Light from the One Light from the Cosmic Womb, we eternally solidify, change form, and solidify once again.

Scientists claim that energy cannot be destroyed; it merely changes form.

Where we can find the number 108, the sesquiquintile:

On the mundane front, my husband and I are movie fans. Some years ago, we watched the film *Bull Durham* about a woman involved with baseball players. I never expected to obtain a piece of information for this book from that film, but indeed, it happened.

In the beginning of the film, as the camera pans a room, the voice of leading actress Susan Sarandon is heard in the background. She is speaking of her search for meaning in life, and she casually mentions that there are 108 beads in a rosary. You can image that my ears perked up when I heard that number. I went to the library the next morning . . . you recall, I wrote this book initially in the late '80s, before the Internet.

As an aside: Baseball analyst for the *Boston Globe*, Alex Speier, uses 108 Stitches as his signature. There are 108 stitches in a baseball.

We were talking about the 108 beads in a rosary. The word "rosary" comes from the Latin "rosarium," meaning "rose garden." Here's another connection to the "sacred garden" found in many myths. Rosaries in all forms are strings of beads or knots used in prayers and devotions. They can be found in widespread use in many religions and may have originated in Hindu India.

The Jain rosaries have 108 beads or multiples of this number. The Sikhs use rosaries of 108 knots or iron beads. In Mahayanna Buddhism, the prayer rope usually has 108 beads. In India, the number of recited names in a litany of the Goddess Mother of the World is 108. The rosary commonly used in the Catholic religion has 50 small beads separated by four large beads (54 x 2=108).

The prayer beads are a way of elevating the soul, keeping oneself centered in a busy world, and maintaining a connection with the teachings of one's religion. By chanting a mantra or prayer over and over while touching each bead, one moves into a trancelike or meditative state, much like that produced by the rhythmic drumbeats in Indian or African rituals.

This meditative state allows one to experience a reality above or beyond the present worldly condition. It reinforces the knowledge that there are two worlds of reality, one that we can see and touch and smell, and another that cannot be seen but is felt and believed in.

This meditative state allows the balancing of heart and mind, when the lion (Leo rules the heart) lies down with the lamb (Aries, the lamb, rules the head). Our religion should bring about this meeting of the head and the heart if our lives are to be full and productive.

A search of the Internet will provide you with more metaphysical food for thought regarding the numbers 72 and 108.

The Great Pyramid:

The Great Pyramid is said to be a mathematical stone message, incorporating celestial and terrestrial measurements in its architecture that embody the relationships between time and the eternal.

Hidden within the measurements of the Great Pyramid is the value of Pi (Π , 3.1415), mentioned earlier as the standard measure of the relationship between the circumference and the diameter of a circle.

The height of the pyramid is to twice its base as one is to 3.1415, Π . The sarcophagus in the main chamber was constructed upon the same Pi proportions; its height is to twice its base as one is to 3.1415.

The Pi value (3.1415):

Frank C. Higgins, in Hermetic Masonry, writes, ". . . the pi proportion is something that is never absent, in one form or other, from every one of the world's primitive religions, and certainly enters deeply and radically into the philosophies that have given rise to what we in these days call 'Masonry'."[1]

Π, 3.1415, is popularly attributed to the Greek mathematician and engineer Archimedes (280 BCE).

Archimedes may have used Pi in 280 BCE but Moses (1,400 BCE), supposed author of Genesis, trained in Egypt by the Masters, also knew the value of Pi and disguised its measurements in the first word for the Old Testament God in the Bible: in the name Elohim or ALHIM.

God as Pi (3.1415):

When reading about the name of God in the first book of the Old Testament in the Christian Bible, keep in mind that the value of Pi (Π, 3.1415) mentioned above is the standard measure of the relationship between the circumference and the diameter of a circle.

In our terms, Pi is the relationship between the circumference of a circle (Spirit) and the diameter of a circle (Matter). In other words, Pi is the relationship between the Spirit and Matter.

The Old Testament in Hebrew reads: "In the beginning, ALHIM created the heaven and the earth . . .". The value of Pi is hidden behind this name.

Keep in mind that zero is not a number but a placeholder, an additive identity; e.g: 30=3+0=3.

Using Hebrew Gematria, we discover that the value behind the letters in the name ALHIM is 3.1415!

See the illustrations that follow:

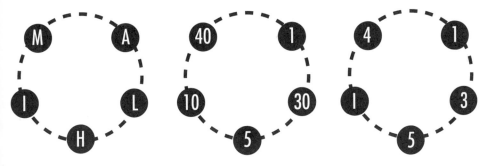

Pi, the name of ALHIM in the first sentence of the Bible, represents the infinite relationship between Spirit and Matter, between the Cosmic Mother and Cosmic Child, between the Creator and you.

Therefore, ALHIM (Elohim) is the constant eternal relationship between Spirit and Matter. ALHIM is the blueprint of the Creator.

The use of the different names of Spirit had to do with the particular activity that was going on at the time; the numbers and geometry behind these names are the clues to what was happening during the formation of the Universe.

God as ALHIM, Elohim, is the blueprint for the construction of life.

God, as Jehovah, is the motion that animates that blueprint.
(See Chapter 4 for a reminder of this connection.)

So, we have the god ALHIM creating the Universe and the god Jehovah giving life to that creation.

Wow! You have to admit this is pretty cool! Doesn't it just get your curious juices flowing, urging you to explore more? Well, let's continue, because there is more.

Old Mother Goddess:

The old Mother Goddess religion approved of sensual pleasure: The new Father God religion disapproved of sensual pleasure. Many other cultures were in tune with the earthiness of the birth processes of the Great Mother.

One can only marvel at current patriarchal interpretations of the emotions of the people who created the figures seen below: Tlazolteotl and a "minor" Hindu female deity.

(I drew these pictures free hand from illustrations I saw in an encyclopedia way back in the days before the Internet.)

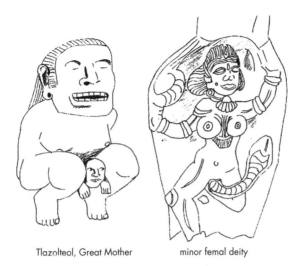

Tlazolteol, Great Mother   minor femal deity

The figure on the left: A Modern Encyclopedia of Symbols reads: "Tlazolteotl, Great Mother of the Aztecs, has none of the celestial aloofness of Isis and Mary, but crouches and grimaces in the travail of birth and creation."

There's no "celestial aloofness" in these drawings; the woman is the Earth Mother in all her glory.

Notice the word "travail," which means "pain, anguish, and suffering." The Christian God decreed that woman shall bring forth life in pain so here we find a biased, traditionally patriarchal interpretation of a woman's experience of the birth process. Perhaps the Great Mother's grimace was one of hard work and joy, or maybe . . . it was a smile! My goodness . . . what a thought!!

The Hindu figure on the right, perhaps Shakti, represents the Great Mother who gave birth to the universe from her Yoni. She could hardly be called a "minor" female deity. In fact, it is contradictory to call her a minor deity while stating that the serpent, a symbol of the basic creative energy of life, is issuing from her vulva. The serpent, snake, and dragon, in all world religions, have great power because these symbols represent the Five vitality that endows humanity with intelligence and life.

In Chapter 4, it was shown that the Sacred Trapezoid diagram is constructed upon the number values of the name Jehovah. We saw how the serpent, snake, and the dragon became symbols of wisdom because of the Sun's serpentine movement over the equator from the Tropic of Cancer to the Tropic of Capricorn on its endless journey in the Earth's history. This passage of time has the potential to bestow wisdom on those with eyes to see. Therefore, in myths and parables, these undulating creatures have evolved to represent wisdom. "Be ye wise as serpents."

In Naomi Goldenberg's book, *The Changing of the Gods*, she suggests replacing the word "deity" with the word "deaty" because it comes from dea, or goddess, the feminine aspect of divinity. It is the female Mother Goddess energy that births life.

The creative energy of the woman was not treated kindly by the early Western church fathers, but other cultures experienced it quite differently. Keep an open mind when reading or examining the thoughts traditionally put forward these last few thousand years, because they are based in patriarchal thinking, the male based fear that has given rise to the subjugation of women.

The ancient cultures worshipped the Great Mother who, alone and unaided (the virgin), brought forth life through Her gateway (the Vesica Piscis) into the world of form.

The Fish:

The fish is associated with the Vesica Piscis and also with the advent of the Piscean Age some 2,000 years ago. In the early days of Christianity, because these early worshippers feared persecution, they would draw a stylized fish in the sand to silently notify those around them of their belief.

This image is still used today. It can be seen on car bumper stickers identifying the driver as a Christian. The last 2,000 years we have been experiencing the Age of Pisces, a water sign symbolized by the fish. We are now on the edge of the 2,000-year period called the Age of Aquarius, so we are entering a new philosophical mind set with different symbols of worship.

Architecture as a Book of History:

Some sacred structures, temples, and churches from the past are the books of history because they contain sacred geometry and sacred numbers that tell the stories the ancients wove into these structures for posterity.

Certainly architecture is a more enduring location to keep the secrets of the past than papyrus, clay tablets, books, and even the Internet.

Communication with the Universe

The most enduring languages are the five universal symbols of geometry and the natural unfolding laws of the first five numbers, those tools in your archeological work kit.

Cosmologist Carl Sagan, in his 1985 novel *Contact*, explored how one could communicate with alien civilizations using prime numbers followed by universal principles of math and science.

*****

That's what I'm saying . . . no matter where you go, a circle is a circle.

Well, you did it! You've read Part I and learned two languages. In the process, you ate the whole box of peanut clusters, but you deserved it.

Now, just like the film industry shows preview teasers for their big blockbuster films about to be released to the public, here's the coming attraction about a really big blockbuster film that's about to be released:

The Delineations of the Quintiles and SesquiQuintiles

Through the Pillars of the 72° aspect you will discover your talent in this lifetime; through the Pillars of the 108° aspect you will leave your legacy for future generations.

Interested? Please read on.

PART II

CHAPTER 1

THE NATURAL ZODIAC
TECHNIQUE AND THE ESSENCE
OF THE HOUSES

In order to understand the meaning of any aspect, we will use the Natural Zodiac as a template. This template represents the complete circle of life that applies to every being on this earth, no matter where you were born or at what time of day.

The Natural Zodiac is what I call the Wheel of Life. The zodiacal wheel begins with 0° at the Spring Equinox, the point of beginnings each year, that moment when the Sun crosses the equator on its northerly journey.

The zodiacal 360° circle is then divided into twelve pie-shaped wedges, which are the houses. These houses are the tools we will use to understand the basic meaning of the quintile and sesquiquintile.

In Rob Hand's book, *Planets in Transit*, he writes about a method of aspect analysis used in India. This method looks at each aspect through the houses that come into play when starting from the point of beginnings, the first house.

He writes: "The conjunction is considered to be a first-house aspect; the sextile, a third-house, eleventh-house aspect; the square, a fourth-house, tenth-house aspect; the trine, a fifth-house, ninth-house aspect; and the opposition, a seventh-house aspect."

He goes on to write: "The relationship of the houses to the aspects is completely valid as long as one realizes that the houses themselves are merely superficial meanings derived from much more basic principles."[1]

The "more basic principles" are the essences of the houses, not the external activities associated with those houses.

So, rather than look at the third house as siblings, local travel, and hometown newspapers, we need to look at the underlying principle of that house. In this case, the third house is where we first encounter our immediate environment and have to learn how to communicate. This is where our personal thought processes are formed.

To understand the essence of each house, let's take a brief journey through the Wheel of Life starting when we took our first breath.

The First House:

We take our first breath at 0° on the wheel, reminiscent of emerging from the Cosmic Egg. We open our eyes and encounter a new world for the first time. We find ourselves alone in a new strange world, no luggage in hand. All we know is that we exist, we are. We are totally focused on self.

The Second House:

Here we settle into our new body and begin to realize we need certain necessities in order to survive: food and water. A clean bottom is also helpful. Someone takes care of these needs so we feel good about ourselves.

The Third House:

In the second house we learn that if our needs aren't fulfilled, we can find ways to get our message across: crying, kicking our arms and legs, until someone reacts. As mentioned above, this is where we reach out to our immediate environment, to those beings around us, to communicate our personal needs. Here we develop our method of processing information and learning to think and express our thoughts.

The Fourth House:

Now we realize that we belong to a group where one person seems to rule. We learn that we have to share the attention and integrate into this body. This is our harbor of safety, the family.

The Fifth House:

After learning the rules of living within the family dynamic, we feel the urge to express our individuality apart from members of family. We dare to reach out on our own to find our niche through our creative talents. We explore our first loves outside the family unit and the love of things that make us happy.

The Sixth House:

We now learn to develop useful skills around those creative energies from the fifth house. We find that daily routines and a healthy body are necessary to earn our keep and to be of service.

The Seventh House:

We have developed ourselves to the point that we now are ready to step out into the world. Will others accept us? This is the house of one-on-one personal relationships, where we discover who we are through the mirror reflection of the other. This is where we set the tone for all future relationships.

The Eighth House:

After joining with the other, we now have the capacity to create new life. Along with this new life comes the responsibility to gather and protect the resources that will ensure this life will continue.

The Ninth House:

Now that we are responsible for the group we have birthed, we realize that laws must be made to protect the clan. Here our thinking expands to include other groups that need protection. We enact these laws and store them for future reference. The knowledge we have gained along the way informs our belief systems.

The Tenth House:

In our burgeoning civilization, we realize there must be a central core, a leader, an office, a place the public can look to for representation. Here, we also take our place in the sun to receive accolades as we contribute our skills in the public arena.

The Eleventh House:

Once we have contributed to civilization, we look around and ask how can we enjoy the fruits of our labor or how can we use our life's experiences to help others. We may find that humanitarian service is where the true rewards are bestowed.

The Twelfth House:

Here we find our spiritual core, where we desire to serve others without recognition, where we finally realize that we are all One. We have "danced round the ring" and have finally found the Secret that "sits in the middle and knows."

Using this brief discussion of the essence of the houses, let's look at the conjunction and square through the method of aspect analysis discussed above.

In each case, we start at the first house and move in both directions around the wheel.

The Conjunction:

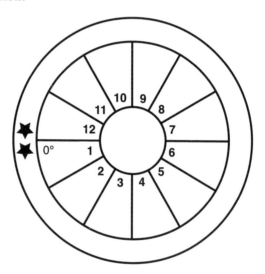

To understand the meaning of the conjunction, regardless of the planets involved, we start at the first house and, because the planets are conjunct, we stay in the first house. This doubles the energy output, increasing their range and impact. Just like the old Doublemint Gum commercial: double the energy; double the fun.

The first house is totally centered on you and how you see things, and rightly so, because the powerful motivation is self-focus and self-awareness. The conjunction is considered a powerful aspect because two energies are joined together; one doesn't leave home without the other.

Planets in conjunction are cosmic twins, linked together through this lifetime. Whatever action one takes, the other is always involved, and vice-versa. The conjunction has the power of your self focus behind it.

The Square:

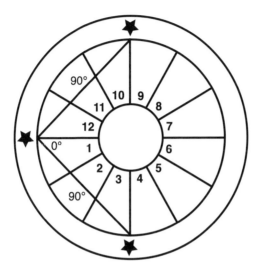

With the square, we start at the first house, then move 90° in a clockwise and a counter-clockwise direction. We find that one leg of the square activates the fourth house and the other leg activates the tenth house.

To understand the meaning of the square, regardless of the planets involved, take into account the meaning of the fourth and tenth houses in relationship to how you see the world, the first house.

The First House View:

Let's face it; when you look at a group photograph in which you are included— even if it's of people you love—who is the first person you search for? It's you! You squint and think: How do I look? Then you decide it's either a good shot of you or you hate it. You either frame it for the wall or it goes into the paper shredder. Well, maybe you're not that violent, but you don't like a bad photo. After examining yourself, you move on to the other people in the photograph.

First house planets in the natal chart do the same thing. Their purpose is to focus on the self; that's self-centered, not selfish. There is a difference. Self-centering is primal; it's survival.

The square is defined as a stress point, because from the first house of autonomy, you are challenged by the fourth and tenth houses, which demand that you conform and meld into the group dynamic. This is a challenge; as a result, you put on your boxing gloves. From the first house combative stance, you are bouncing and weaving and loosening your shoulders, preparing for the big fight.

"No way," you shout out to the crowd! "I'm not giving up my autonomy." It's a battle because it's a one-two punch. You are hit on two fronts.

The Fourth House:

Well, accept it! You do have to find a way to fit into that noisy group in the emotional fourth house, because it's your family, after all. You do have to listen to one particular authority figure (your Mother) and give up your autonomy. You will be absorbed into that unit where you must compete for attention with those other family members who are so clingy, while you still try to maintain your identity. You don't know if you like this connection because it's going to require major adjustments in your lifestyle.

The stress meter's in red.

This stressful adjustment takes place in the privacy of your home where the interactions with family members, and life under the rule of Mom's law, will help you construct the foundation upon which your life will be built. As the poet wrote, in honor of Mothers: "The hand that rocks the cradle is the hand that rules the world" (William Ross Wallace).

The Tenth House:

The tenth house is another challenge to your autonomy! You're also stressed here because this house requires that you follow the rules in the very structured house of career, where you are in the public eye and where you have to live by the rules of society set by the accomplished authorities who preceded you. If you're to succeed in terms of the world's assessment of you, if you want to reach that mountain top, you have to follow long-established rules. You don't like that restriction; you want to live by your own rules. Unlike the fourth house where you can work out these issues behind closed doors, this adjustment takes place in the public eye, in the tenth house, where everyone can see you!

You can see why the one-two punch of the square is so stressful. It requires that you give up some of your autonomy, your self-centeredness, in order to interact with the inner world of the family to build a secure foundation for your life, and it also requires that you give up some of your autonomy so that you can find your place in the outer world where society judges your actions.

Again, the stress meter is in the red zone. The square is a call to action.

You can apply this technique of house analysis to the sextile, trine, and opposition as well. In fact, you can apply this technique to any aspect that falls within the zodiacal wheel.

We are going to use this technique to understand the meaning of the quintile and the sesquiquintile.

CHAPTER 2

THE STRUCTURE
AND DEFINITION OF
THE QUINTILE

The quintile separates planets by an orb of 72°.

Using the technique described in the previous chapter to understand the meaning of the quintile, start at zero degrees on the Natural Zodiac. Count 72° in both directions around the wheel. One leg of the aspect will fall in the third house while the other leg falls in the tenth house. Therefore, the meaning of the quintile connects your personal view of the world with the essence of these two houses.

See the diagram below.

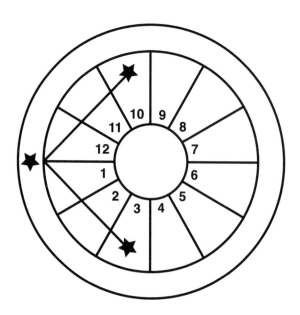

The Third House Leg:

The quintile has some of the qualities of the sextile aspect in the sense that one leg of the quintile activates the third house.

The basic meaning of the third house is the process by which you learn to make sense of your immediate surroundings, how your inner world makes connections with your outer environment, and because of this, how you learn to articulate your personal thoughts learned from this interaction, independently of others.

From out of your individual thought process, your mind creates. Thoughts are things. With dedicated application, what you think and believe can come true because your mind is your strength—philosophers claim that the Universe is "mind stuff"—and your personal message can result in a concrete accomplishment that can be heard and recognized in your life through the quintile's tenth house connection.

The Tenth House Leg:

This leg of the quintile falls in the tenth house. This house represents the top of the mountain, your destiny point in this lifetime where your personal ideas and actions are registered in the public consciousness. This is where you have a panoramic view of your life's achievements and where the public judges you.

Your actions may be performed in private, but they will eventually come into the light of the tenth house. Or your work can be very public, seen by the outside world on a daily basis where everyone knows your name and your face.

Therefore, the quintile reveals your ability to structure your personal thoughts in your own creative manner, the third house, and then present them in full view to the world, the tenth house. The quintile is your hidden talent that should be revealed this lifetime, bestowing upon you some form of recognition and fame.

Or infamy! What's your pleasure? I know some of you are naughty!

The quintile has an underlying flavor of Mercury (ruler of the third house) and Saturn (ruler of the tenth house), which reveals your mental versatility, your talent for concretizing your personal visions, and for giving a clear voice to your personal thoughts for public consumption.

Built into our brains is the evolutionary compulsion to share. This drive to share, to belong to the tribe, ensured the survival of our species on many levels. In evolutionary terms, this results in mating, ensuring that our species will continue.

In the brain, the frontal cortex is the region of higher thought. When we talk about ourselves, when we are asked questions about ourselves, two other regions of the brain are activated that release a chemical called dopamine. This chemical opens the "reward pathways"; it makes us feel good. It's the same high that comes with using cocaine and eating chocolate. And it motivates us to want more; it's addictive.

So conversations, sharing personal thoughts and information about ourselves, self-promotion, all these activities create a pleasant high. This can bring us personal recognition, an elevation of our status in the group, which draws others to us.

The quintile represents the pleasure you derive in your creative thoughts, the focus on how you think, and the conversations that empower your ideas. This act results in your finding a public platform from which you will receive the satisfaction that feeds your sense of well being, where you can be recognized in this lifetime as a generational figure.

If you've been wandering around the house wondering where your life is going . . . or if you're slouched at your desk wondering if there isn't something more to your life . . . or you're sprawled on the couch listlessly channel surfing . . . or even if you've just reached an unbelievable goal but now you're wondering what's next . . . it's time to crystallize your hidden talents and show them to the world!

Through the quintile, you have the ability to give voice to your personal creative ideas. Through focusing your mind, you discover that thoughts are things. Those things you achieve can lead you on the path to career recognition where your message can be heard.

CHAPTER 3

THE STRUCTURE
AND DEFINITION OF THE
SESQUIQUINTILE

As described in Part II, Chapter 1, we will use the Natural Zodiac as a template to understand the sesquiquintile. If you haven't read that section, you might want to do so now before you go on.

The sesquiquintile separates planets by 108°.

To find this aspect on the Natural Zodiac, start at 0° and count 108° in both directions around the wheel. One leg of the aspect will fall in the fourth house, while the other leg falls in the ninth house. Therefore, the meaning of the sesquiquintile blends the essence of these two houses.

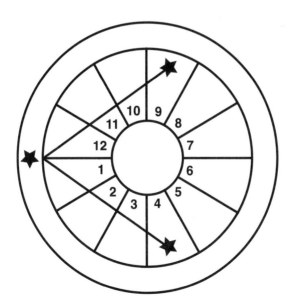

A thorough understanding of the fourth and ninth houses is essential to understand the underlying essence of the sesquiquintile.

The Fourth House Leg:

Because of the fourth house influence, there is a deep motivation to crystallize the creative energy you already possess so that you carry on your ancestral lineage, your inherited DNA, by leaving your mark in the halls of history to inspire following generations.

On the observable level in this lifetime, the fourth house is the human family you are born into. In the best of worlds it is replete with parents, siblings, cats and dogs, and pet geckos. This is where you argue with your siblings, fight for the last warm dinner roll, and protect your little brother from the neighborhood bully. Or you may be a singleton, the object of hovering attention from parents and grandparents and Aunt Alice and Uncle Henry who slobber you with kisses . . . even in front of your friends . . . much to your youthful embarrassment.

The fourth house is the type of home you first live in—a one-story bungalow, a three-room apartment, a soaring steel-and-glass structure, a cabin in the woods, or a yurt by a gurgling stream—a home that is embedded in your memory as a place of comfort and safety. In this private hidey-hole you learn how to nurture through the nurturing you receive from those around you.

The fourth house is the foundation of your life. Sometimes you have to rebuild or abandon your original foundation, fill in the cracks, shore up the timbers, or tear it down and start over again. That works too. You have the blueprint and the hammer and nails built into your DNA memory with which to construct your new home, your base of operations for your current incarnation.

This leg of the sesquiquintile goes deep into the roots of the fourth house. This is the home of the Mother. It is the Mother DNA whose influence was expressed, as mentioned earlier, in the poem, "The hand that rocks the cradle is the hand that rules the world" (Wallace). The fourth house connects you to your particular family tree, the roots of which wind back to the beginning of time. Your deeply buried need to manifest your talent comes from these roots, from your family history, the DNA you inherited and which flows through your every cell. You carry the DNA of your ancestors. The fourth house is your pre-history.

In 1987, a worldwide survey of human mitochondrial DNA, which is passed only from mother to daughter, determined that "all mitochondrial DNAs stem from one woman"[1] who lived around 200,000 years ago in Africa. She is the "Mitochondrial Eve" or "African Eve," sometimes dubbed "Lucy." She is the Mother of us all.

DNA stands for deoxyribonucleic, the double helix of genetic material inherited from ancestors. Mitochondrial comes from the Greek: Mito means thread, and chondrion means grain like granule. Your mitochondrial DNA is the thread that has been woven through your prehistory and is now waiting for you to weave that thread into the cloak you will don in the halls of history.

The Ninth House Leg:

The other leg of the sesquiquintile rests in the ninth house.

The sesquiquintile has some of the same qualities as the trine because one leg is posited in the ninth house. This implies talent, but rather than being casual and perhaps lazy about your abilities as the trine can be, there is that deep fourth house desire that motivates you to crystallize your creative energy.

The ninth house collects and codifies universal thought patterns. Where the third house is our personal method of learning how to communicate with our immediate environment through our thinking process, the ninth house collects our thoughts along with the thoughts of all others in the world.

It is here in the ninth house that we preserve these collected thoughts, which were carved into cave walls, impressed on clay tablets, written on papyri and scrolls, painted in the geometry of great art, and woven into the designs of fabrics and into books and codified laws.

The great library of the ninth house becomes the source of knowledge from which we have the ability to discover how other cultures think. We publish books that spread the Word; we create the laws that protect the diversity of different cultures; we build educational institutions that teach us about the world; we create religions that reflect our beliefs; we physically travel to other cultures to learn more. It is here that future generations can learn from the accumulated knowledge of the past.

It is through the ninth house we develop our belief systems.

This is also the house of prophecy where the more psychic and intuitive amongst us, from that global pool of knowledge, can tap into the thought trends of the world before they are obvious to the general public. The ninth house plants the seed ideas for trends and inventions, and allows a peek into future historical events.

The ninth house leg of the sesquiquintile is our library card into the preserved knowledge of the world and is the key to where our fourth house DNA talent should add to that pool of global knowledge.

The connection between the fourth house depth of instinctual understanding and ninth house pool of knowledge offered to the world defines the sesquiquintile aspect. This aspect provides a treasure map with the Moon (ruler of the fourth house) and Jupiter (ruler of the ninth house) as the keys.

Imagine that the X on the map marks the spot where the treasure is buried. That treasure is your Moon, which holds your Akashic records, the memory of everything you were: the thoughts, actions, and accomplishments of your past, perhaps even a record of your past lives.

You are the continuing thread from that past that will weave your DNA treasure into the future fabric of knowledge. Your talent lies in digging up your pre-existing treasure to expose the gems therein to the world, not only locally but mainly globally. The dig may require effort until that golden moment of discovery when your creative treasure is revealed.

You are the archaeologist using old maps, inscriptions, carvings left by your past, which now direct you to travel to the future, to explore and widen the view, to open broad paths to education and inspiration, to renew the faith of the world through your chosen venue.

The sesquiquintile aspect reveals your personal treasure of pre-existing knowledge. It is the platform upon which to present your unique talent and vision to the world.

You have a deep emotional need to nurture your roots, to concretize what you already know, so that your efforts will bloom in the ninth house of knowledge as a legacy for future generations. You are here to let the world know, to expand the world's beliefs of what is possible through the spread of knowledge.

The sesquiquintile describes the continuing thread of your ancestry and how it has woven the fabric of your current lifetime. This also applies to those who believe in some form of reincarnation, who believe that their past lives have an effect upon their present conditions in this lifetime.

With the sesquiquintile, you might, in the still hours of the night, hear a soft voice calling to you as if from a distance, a message from someone on your Cosmic Family Tree, as I did one memorable night years ago.

It was closing on two in the morning. My four school-aged children were tucked safely in their beds asleep, my husband snoring softly beside me, as I lay in our bed under the comforter. The only light dispelling the darkness came from the bedside gooseneck lamp puddling on the open pages of a book I held in my hands, a book titled *Flatland*, a humorous story about a two-dimensional world populate by circles, triangles, squares, and straight lines. This book is a social commentary on the strict morals of the Victorian era, written by the ninteenth-century mathematician Edwin Abbott Abbott.

Suddenly, as I was reading, a wave of emotion swept over me. With both hands, I drew the book to my chest as tears filled my eyes. This man, dead for a hundred years, had reached across time and space and touched my soul.

This is the power of the sesquiquintile.

It is now fifty years later, and as I reach the end of my journey, I rewrite this book in the hopes that you will find a quiet corner to make your own, where you can read and journey with me through magical lands with your map of numbers and geometry in hand to discover and eventually drink from the golden bowls of the two most powerful astrological aspects, the quintile and sesquiquintile.

I also hope that this book will reach across time and space so that you too will have an emotional moment when you will clasp it to your heart and murmur softly, "Eureka."

Through the sesquiquintile, you are here to dig up your DNA treasure, to solidify that light in the halls of memory so that future generations can also whisper in the wee hours of the morning, "Eureka."

PART III

Throughout the following delineations of both the quintiles and the sesquiquintiles, I have used both instructional text and imagery. Rather than memorizing keywords that describe what an aspect means, the visuals leave a greater impact. They evoke emotions from deep within and leave a lasting impression. The interpretations that follow are a combination of show and tell: The visuals show; the analysis tells. Just like in school—show and tell. I love it!

The imagery contains a bit of hyperbole and often humor. It is my nature to paint big pictures to further impress the meanings of the aspects. I do want you to remember your aspects!

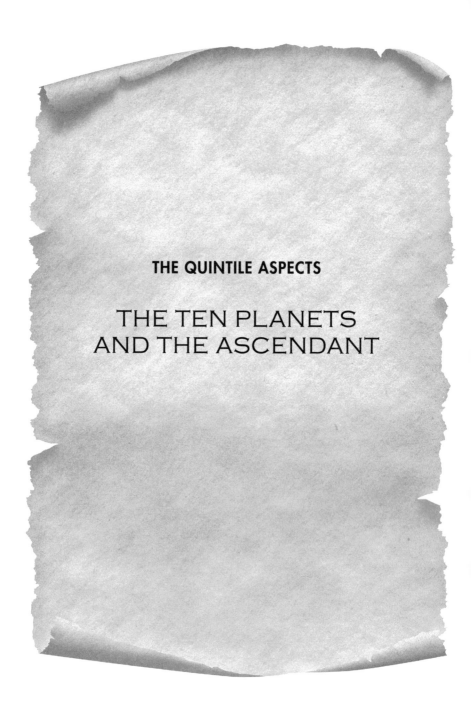

THE QUINTILE ASPECTS

THE TEN PLANETS
AND THE ASCENDANT

THE MOON SPEAKS TO YOUR EMOTIONS AND NURTURING INSTINCT

☽ Q ☉ **Moon quintile Sun:**
Your Career Message:
Be the Big Mama.

Your Hidden Talent:
Your welcoming smile casts sunshine wherever you go. A bright smile, a warm embrace, a bend of the knee to wipe away the tears of a small child, these things comes naturally to you. Your aura radiates this quiet sensitivity and strength. In this sense, you are a healer.

Your hidden talent is your ability to make people feel at ease and comforted in your presence. Your natural comfort level with both women and men is the result of your ability to identify with the inherent traits in both sexes.

Others sense your acceptance and your strength, and they feel they can confide in you about their most personal problem. You instinctively know what they need to hear. You find the right words, which you convey in a calm, respectful voice. As a result, others feel better about themselves.

Your role as the Big Mama/Big Papa figure can bring recognition from the public and place you in a position of power in almost any field you want to pursue. You carry the mantle of leadership and that, along with your calm presence, evokes trust from others.

Your inner resources are fed by the pool of your life experiences. You draw upon this internal library and are able to express your thoughts fluently. Professions that require a quick mind and a nurturing hand are home for you. You are here to use your talent as a natural leader. You can be a recognized figure in your community for your love of home and country. Also, you will be recognized for the easy way you interact and nurture others. You're the calm voice at the contentious school meetings, the accessible and friendly CEO of a diversified food company, the cook at the local diner whose friendly ear encourages others to write an inspirational novel. Or you could write that inspirational novel!

Your emotional needs and your ego needs are good friends, enjoying a comfortable alliance. You are here to use these balanced strengths to spread joy along your path to recognition in your chosen career.

Moon quintile Mercury:
Your Career Message:
Stock silver pens.

Your Hidden Talent:
You have the imagination of a great thinker who stirs the emotions of the public. Because you are emotionally comfortable with your thoughts, your words flow like liquid night, sailing across the star-studded heavens of your mind. You are here to inspire others to find their creative voice.

Yes, you are the poet, the imaginative writer, the dreamer, but you're not so starry-eyed that you get nothing done. You have the ability to translate your imagination into practical action.

Your good memory serves you well; you can draw upon stored information from your past experiences. Like a computer or well-organized filing cabinet, your psychic antenna has quick access to that internal library. Because of this, your conversations are tactful, easily conveyed, and understood, and touch the heart of the matter at hand.

Your talent, like cream, rises to the top. From this position, you can use your ability to understand the details and, with your willingness to work, you gain the respect of those around you. You are the spokesperson who captures the minds of the audience, perhaps through tossing in a bit of poetic license to stimulate the imagination of the group.

You sense the feelings of others, which aides your instinctual sense of timing. You know when to hold them and when to fold them, the best attributes of a good business head. You have the key to success, which is timing! Plant five healthy tomato plants in the best soil in a sunny garden and, with tender care, you can expect success . . . unless, that is, you plant the tender seedlings in the harsh winters of northern Montana.

Also, you innately understand that diet, cleanliness, and good health are necessary parts of your life. Your purpose in life may revolve around teaching these values as a fitness guru or the owner of a health food business; whatever you do, you have an instinctual ability to convey your message in such a way that the public knows that you speak from experience.

You make your mark in this world through a career that allows your creative communication skills to stir the emotion and imagination of the public in ways that nurture and provide comfort. Where's that pen?

Moon quintile Venus:
Your Career Message:
Hug a puppy.

Your Hidden Talent:
You "walk in beauty, like the night of cloudy climes and starry skies." There is a part of you that feels a deep need for romance. Supported by your emotional instincts and needs in relationships, you are here to express the soul of a poet.

Your talent is that you instinctively know how to relate to others; you know when to listen and when to lend a gentle touch to the relationship. Your goal is sharing a happy and harmonious partnership, complete with visions of floating off on moonbeams in a loving embrace.

One of the most creative of all the quintiles in the artistic sense, this connection you have between your inner soul and your outer vision of beauty can also manifest in delicately touching pieces of art and music. The Yin side of you is powerful and strong.

Your nurturing instincts seek a peaceful environment in which to live and work. You are willing and very able to discuss challenges in your search for settling differences.

Women figure importantly in your life, and your connections with them create a strong sisterhood, a support system throughout your life. You may be an advocate for women's issues.

You are woman; you are strong. You can hold positions of authority, not through brute strength but through a gentle hand. However, people should not underestimate your charming and affectionate nature or view your femininity as an invitation to dismiss your capabilities; big mistake! You are the figure that others look up to as the power of the woman. Women rule . . . as seen by tiny goddess statues found all over the ancient world.

Coupled with your natural curiosity and a good business sense, you can find power in home, family, and domestic pursuits as well as business pursuits that serve these areas. The role of artist and peacekeeper can be your claim to fame.

Beneath it all is your pool of creative talent that seeks expression in all that is beautiful. Your gentle soul is your path to recognition and success. When all is said and done, love is the answer.

☽ Q ♂   Moon quintile Mars:
Your Career Message:
Jump-start your imagination.

Your Hidden Talent:
An emotional spark plug, you are an instigator. That is meant in the nicest possible way, of course. Your enormous emotional energy keeps everyone on their toes. You react to circumstances with drive and willpower. Clear the pathway, for you're driving head-first on all cylinders while keeping an eye out for any stray chipmunks crossing your path.

While others meet challenges huffing and puffing . . . I think I can, I think I can . . . you're dreaming about being at the top of the hill, exclaiming "I already did!" You are here to become that engine pulling the train.

You can prove that, with an emotional charge, it can be done. Your energetic personality along with your charm makes you the most noticeable person to get the job done. You have uncanny instincts when it comes to fixing things. You dig into your subconscious library for the instruction manuals and proceed from there.

You want personal contact with people because the interactions light your fires. When you're fired up, you may startle people at first but you also set them at ease with your ability to explain yourself in a caring manner. From positions of authority, you nurture others through stimulating conversations that manage to get things done for the benefit of all.

Moon oriented professions are in your comfort zone. The Moon rules writers, the ocean, women, children, home and family, cooks and restaurants, the environment, and sleep. You may do your best work in bed! Through your dreams. What were you thinking?

You're the fiery advocate for saving the whales or for the rights of women and their children. You could cook a mean seared scallops with jalapeno vinaigrette and win the coveted James Beard Award, or you may find inspiration in your dreams when you awake in the dark of night fumbling for your notebook so you can scribble the messages darting in and out of your head, hoping you can read what you wrote in the light of day. See, that's what is meant about doing your best work in bed!

Whether you work in the dark of night or in the blazing Sun, you can be seen as the one who accomplishes her goals. You are here to reign from the mountaintop as the go-to gal.

☽ Q ♃

Moon quintile Jupiter:
Your Career Message:
Exceed your grasp.

Your Hidden Talent:

As the poet Browning wrote: "Your reach should exceed your grasp or what's a heaven for?" Your talent is your imagination that soars into higher realms of knowledge where you find comfort in the libraries populated with the accumulated wisdom of the past. Your intellectual curiosity is backed by your capacity to absorb and store enormous amounts of information.

So, you're not just a talking head; you know what you're talking about. You instinctively understand the emotional needs of the world for growth towards something better. You have great sympathy for those who are considered less fortunate, and you could become the spokesperson for campaigns that address the need for opportunities that will open doors for those who wish to exceed their grasp. You help others because it is in your generous nature to do so.

You stress the value of ethics and honesty. You could express this vision through the halls of justice, through the arts, through teaching, writing, and speaking. In business, your urge to nurture the growth potential of others may find a home in the area of domestic services. Your vision of what is possible inspires others to reach for something bigger and better.

From a position of leadership, you could be seen as a person whose integrity and honesty are never in question. As a result, your influence could result in great achievements; you seek to accomplish more. As Teddy Roosevelt wrote: "Far better it is to dare mighty things . . . [than to] live in a gray twilight than knows not victory nor defeat."

You dream and can achieve mighty things because you instinctively understand how to assemble pieces of information; your "knowing" borders on prophecy. Your ability to comprehend the direction of the public's attention, to see what they want before they know what they want, supports the success of any business enterprise upon which you might embark. You know what sells.

You are here to use your insights and broad view of the world in whatever profession you choose. Your good will could extend to other countries and provide welcome to other cultures. You can be recognized in your lifetime as a trusted leader with a big vision who made positive contributions to help others exceed their grasp.

☽ Q ♄ **Moon quintile Saturn:**
Your Career Message:
Build stone walls.

Your Hidden Talent:
Like the farmer in Robert Frost's "Mending Wall," you instinctively know and respect the rules that are necessary in a civilized society if life is to continue in a manner that supports everyone. You are here to demonstrate that you can be comfortable within the marble halls constructed by your predecessors. These hallowed places have withstood the vicissitudes of time and they continue to preserve and protect. You are here to build more stone walls through the constructive use of your imagination.

Your talent is your practical approach to your work, along with the conservation of resources. You can surprise others whose deadlines stretch endlessly like the Amazon River winding through overgrown jungles and muddy tangled waters where sweat and tears often result in failure. You don't waste time. You know how to organize projects, set up a timeline, and diligently follow that timeline to its productive end. For this, you can be recognized.

Whereas some people do the same thing over and over expecting a success that never comes—the definition of insanity—you do it once because you have thoroughly planned it well beforehand.

Serious and levelheaded, you can rule from a place of power in your given field. You are seen as one who wears the crown of integrity.

Others should not expect bubbly and sparkly from you, except when they toast your accomplishments. And that's just fine. They need your common sense and reserved cautious attitude.

You maintain the status quo yet build upon it. You're not a daydreamer; you're a day builder. You stand amongst those who give concrete expression to their creative imagination. When you dream, most likely you never leave your neighborhood because you find comfort within those perimeters. Fences and boundaries provide a safe place to nurture your imagination.

You may find yourself in varied professions from the law and politics to the domestic and social services. Whether you babysit a bevy of babies in your preschool establishment or you babysit your country as a defender of justice, you can be honored for your integrity, preparedness, and steadfast determination in the service of others.

Moon quintile Uranus:
Your Career Message:
Ride the moon beams.

Your Hidden Talent:
You are here to stand in the rarified air of the mountaintop as the emotional conscience of freedom. It started when you were a baby, throwing off restraining clothing, complaining at the top of your lungs when you were shushed, and generally causing havoc at unusual times and in the most inappropriate places.

Your curiosity and independent thinking, fueled by dissent, make you an employer's nightmare, so you might as well face it. You need to be on top of the pile, or you need to work alone where your inventive mind can have free reign.

You don't do things the way others do; you are different. Way different, and viva la difference! You can't and won't be hampered by rules that make no sense to you. You do have an advantage, however, in that you can use your calming demeanor to soothe the savage beast of denial in others.

Even though your ideas and actions are way outside the box, you are here to achieve a position in society where you are able to coax others outside that box with you . . . although with the more conservative types, it may be only a little bit outside . . . However, that's a step in the right direction as far as you are concerned.

At first, they'll be aghast, denying and disputing your ideas, but eventually, as the reality sets in that you are right, they begin to see the light. Your ingenuity shines the light and your ideas become recognized as normal.

Speaking of normal, that you aren't. One definition of normal is being devoid of any outstanding characteristics. No one with the stretchiest imagination would describe you that way. You're a free thinker and that's good for all of us! The world needs unfettered thinkers, those *Star Trek* warriors who go where no one has gone before, in order to open new paths to the future.

You stand up for your gay classmate in grade school and later for the rights of women around the world. You challenge the accepted scientific theories of the day and pave the way for interior and exterior space exploration.

You can be recognized in this life as one amongst that rare group who break "the-ring-pass-not" with your innovative thinking.

95

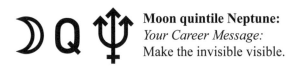

Moon quintile Neptune:
Your Career Message:
Make the invisible visible.

Your Hidden Talent:

You are a mystic and poet who is here to use your gift with words to inspire the romance in life. Your imagination takes you on angel wings into the "Mists of Avalon." Marion Zimmerman Bradley's novel of the same name tells the story of King Arthur's legend through the eyes of women. Your creative talent lies in the nurturing feminine, in the land of sleep and dreams, mysticism, and spirituality. You are here to use your imagination as a canvas upon which to paint your Neptunian visions.

You need time alone in spaces where fairies play and fantasy reigns. Your talent is inspired beside a hidden woodland stream flowing over moss-covered rocks or by a quiet pond nestled in the forested hills or by the fog shrouded shores of a gently lapping ocean upon a secretive cove. Or even beside the aquarium next to your desk. Regardless of the form it takes, you need water, not just as the necessary liquid of life but as the medium that stimulates your inner talent. Water draws you into its embrace and then gently births you out.

After a day of pressures, social interactions, and world news, you need a bath rather than a shower to dissolve the clinging detritus. Slipping into a warm tub—lightly scented with flowery salts, surrounded by flickering pink and white candles, the "Moonlight Sonata" playing in the background—is the rejuvenating sanctuary for your soul.

Then you're ready for the next day when you can once again reach out to people through your soothing words and acceptance of all manner of folk. You might write romantic verse for a greeting card company, or pen a fantasy novel. You may visit kindergartens, hospitals, and nursing homes, where you can weave stories that enchant others. Your presence alone is the healing energy between this world and the next.

You tune in to the unseen subtle forces of a world beyond the physical, which stimulates your psychic and mediumistic abilities. You are here to make the invisible visible.

You may keep a diary where you record your dreams each morning because it is within this nebulous realm where the mysteries reside, where you are in touch with the vast imagination as you sail the creative waters of your soul.

Moon quintile Pluto:
Your Career Message:
Conjure up your magic.

Your Hidden Talent:

You are the witchy woman, dancing naked under a silvery full Moon while your witch's coven casts spells on the landscape. A cohort of the Earth Mother, you are intimate with the magnetic lines of this Earth. You are here to use your talent as a chemist plucking hidden plants from the boggy soil to prepare rejuvenating elixirs. You are here to show your magic to the world.

You are the nurse who reaches deep into her medicinal memory and withdraws the perfect remedy for the patient, the mother who takes over the failing septic company and remakes it into a successful business, the CEO who brings her whole foods company back from the dead.

Your talent for breathing new life into crumbling lives and fortunes, for recycling the detritus of the past, is truly powerful.

Your voice may be heard through local newspapers, publications, or journals where your passion almost seeps through the pages. If you write a poem, it's not Elizabeth Barrett Browning, it's Edgar Allen Poe . . . deep, dark, intense, transforming . . . because you feel that in your soul.

Intimacy is profound and meaningful. Sex is a spiritual ritual, a transforming act where you both understand that love is more than just copulating, more than just chocolates and roses. You want one soul mate with whom you can experience the intensity of sharing your life.

You also have an uncanny instinct to sense the falsehoods in others. Your eyes narrow, your breathing slows, your eyes peer into the other persons intentions. As a therapist, you draw out rudimentary truths from your clients. They can't hide anything from you.

You are the instinctive detective, drawing from your velvet black bag of magic, to the surface, that which was hidden.

Whatever profession you choose—from the mother that rocks the cradle to the mother that rules the world—your job is to be recognized as a healer who transforms your world through deep fundamental change.

☽ Q ASC

Moon quintile Ascendant:
Your Career Message:
Record your dreams.

Your Hidden Talent:

You have an instinctive awareness of the emotions of others, and you can adjust accordingly. You are here to use your natural talent to sympathize and be sensitive to the needs of those around you, to provide others with a safe and comfortable environment while they are in your presence.

Your brain is always active; it never stops figuring and refiguring. You unconsciously absorb the patterns in the environment around you; you feel the things that you experience. It's a simple next step to understand those same patterns in others. Therefore, you instinctively comprehend the needs of those around you, and you respond with a nurturing embrace.

You are a natural when working with the public because you pick up on the current moods of the time and of the day. You display your sensitivity naturally, which invites other people into your world. Your instinctive reaction and quick thinking suggests that your skills could be used through the media as a talk show host, a newscaster, a therapist, or as a writer. You know what makes people tick. You might even have a daily Moon guide at hand to confirm your reading of the public's mood on any given day.

Your conversational life is fluid. Your active mind easily accesses the information you store daily so you are able to converse with people on many subjects. You pull up the tidbits that fit the topics under discussion.

You want to be there on the scene when there is a need. Your profession may be expressed through the healing professions as a doctor, a nurse, or a first responder, because you want to be actively involved.

Your hidden talent is your ability to find solutions to problems from your dreams. You would be wise to keep a dream journal in which to record your dreams each morning. There will be plenty of inspiration to draw from because your creative subconscious mind dances and twirls through multiple landscapes gathering the information needed to reach logical conclusions.

Through your career choice, you can be publicly recognized for your warm personality that draws people into your orb, people who benefit from your instinct to jump into the fray and take care of those in need, emotionally or physically.

THE SUN SPEAKS TO YOUR IDENTITY

☉ Q ♂   **Sun quintile Mars:**
Your Career Message:
Be the light of courage.

Your Hidden Talent:
The drive embedded in your identity marks you as the person who has the courage to step in when things need to get done. You are the spark plug that initiates activity, the one that others will follow because of your confidence and your ability to communicate your goals. This is your inborn talent that needs to be externalized.

You are not afraid of work; in fact, you work harder than most people, and you enjoy it at the same time. Plus, you don't spin your wheels and go nowhere. You work intelligently; you know what you're doing, unlike many others who are all talk and no action. You can explain your process in direct, simple terms so that others follow your line of reasoning. This is a direct result of your interest in learning. You will never be the old dog that can't learn new tricks.

Your strong will manifests in your desire to accomplish your objectives. You have a comfortable itch that you continually scratch, stimulating you on to new projects. Your actions inspire others to follow you. As a dynamic leader, you can motivate others through your example.

You have a competitive side, but it's expressed in a manner that doesn't arouse the defenses of others; rather, it draws people to you and your cause.

Your search for new vistas of information suits you for dangerous adventures into places that others would not venture. Your treks may take you into the communication professions such as public relations, teaching, dynamic writing, and reporting. Investigation might also be your bailiwick.

Recognition can be bestowed upon you for taking decisive and well-planned action in your career, whatever that may be. Your authoritative voice is your "work made visible."

Others will be amazed at the ease with which you accomplish goals, but that is because you actively pursue them with self-confidence. You know where to find it, how to do it, and when to do it. Your uncanny sense of timing is your strength. You are here to inspire others to be adventurous, to do what others dare not do, and to approach life with courage.

☉ Q ♃

Sun quintile Jupiter:
Your Career Message:
Be the light of knowledge.

Your Hidden Talent:

Your talent is your faith and generous nature, which is supported by your inner confidence and the easy ability with which you communicate with others. You are here to take your talents to higher levels and use them from a position of leadership where you can influence others.

Perennially positive, you possess a font of knowledge that is impressive. "Knowing" is not always a key to success, but you have the insight to use your knowledge to guide others in ways that don't threaten them. They understand that you willingly share because you know doing so benefits everyone.

Your vast knowledge comes from understanding the social complexities of the world. You may be an armchair traveler or a world explorer but you have traveled! Whether it's mentally, through studies, or physically, by trains, planes, and automobiles, you have gathered experience that places you in a position of respect. From this public place, you can teach others what you know.

You understand the dangers of the expansion of knowledge without the depth of understanding, as written by author D. W. Buffa in *Rubicon*. You need to obtain a public platform from which to spread your knowledge, the message that all belief systems should have a voice that deserves respect for their identities.

You are not so much concerned with the daily activities of life as you are with the larger concepts that give voice to greater concepts that justify, honor, and protect the smaller voices.

Your talent lies in your love of ideas, philosophies, and the ideologies of the world; you understand how they form a cohesiveness that results in laws that ultimately protect and respect intellectual differences. You present this face in non-threatening positive and welcoming dialogues through your everyday interactions.

This approach to life can place you in positions of respect and authority from which you teach, preach, write, publish, discuss, and legislate your beliefs for the betterment of society. You feel it's your responsibility to give a universal voice to just precepts. You are the ethical voice of society.

Sun quintile Saturn:
Your Career Message:
Be the light of responsibility.

Your Hidden Talent:
You are here to be an example of the serious authority who is respected because of your solid contributions to life. Your practical abilities serve you well in the worlds of business and politics where you build strong foundations.

But you're not the CEO who sits in an ivory tower, above the fray, looking down on the "little people." You understand the cautious steps it takes to build a career, a company, and you trust the processes of those who came before you. Your career is solid because you build it upon the structural bones of the past that have withstood the tests of time.

You know how to talk to those in your employ; you speak their language, encouraging them to reach their goals. Words don't flow from your mouth with sweet promises like some others. You are cautious in discussions, focusing on common-sense approaches. Because of this, you can gain the respect of your business and community, perhaps even beyond because your reach is wide.

Amongst the competitive hard scrabble world of business, you are known as honest and dependable, a rare commodity but one well deserved. Your hard-working ethic is a beacon that draws others. Your discipline and clear leadership skills can be recognized as valuable because they support the institutions upon which the outside world is constructed.

You are serious and methodical about your work, which increases your organizational skills. You can run a meeting with great efficiency; however, you're confident enough to stand in the background and let someone else conduct the meeting if required. Even so, from your back-seat position, you're still a powerful and stable presence in the room.

Whether you exercise your considerable management skills in business, in the legal profession, running a home for the elder community, or commanding an army, you do it with efficiency and integrity.

You combine a rock-steady presence with an inner self-esteem that inspires others. You are hands-on, and your recognition will come from a profession through which you inspire confidence and trust.

Sun quintile Uranus:
Your Career Message:
Be the light of originality; rock the world.

Your Hidden Talent:

Your hidden talent does not suggest but rather shouts that you are different, that you lead the band that marches to a different drummer. Rules? What are those? Some are valid but, if in your mind those rules impinge on freedom of expression, you are here to fix them, to show that it's okay to break the rules in order to accomplish worthwhile goals. However, you're one of those rebels who knows how far to go to break through those walls.

Your quick intuition and originality allows you to see the steps from seed to bloom with lightning quick speed, far surpassing the thought processes of most people. You are quantum leaps ahead of the world in general.

But rather than upset others by challenging their traditional views of the world, your friendly and open manner in conveying your inventive ideas doesn't upset their ingrained traditions. You're always ready to engage in witty intelligent conversation that convinces others to edge a bit more your way.

It's time to bring your light out from under the barrel. You need to shine as the inventor, the one who is unafraid to look at the world differently, and to stand up for and focus your beam on those differences for the benefit of society as a whole. Your ideas and perhaps an invention from your scientific mind could change the world.

You light up the world with your unique personality and lifestyle. People are drawn to you because they know that you don't judge them because of their beliefs or lifestyle; you are open and accepting, and you cast sparkle into your conversations. Your magnetic persona puts you high on the party list.

You are Peter Pan and the Greek god Uranus, wrapped up in one big birthday gift to the world. How boring this place would be without you!

You are the strong progressive leader, the head of movements that open the eyes of the world through not only your inventive ideas but through your popularity, charm, and quirkiness. You don't fit into the "normal" mode; in spite of this, or perhaps because of this, the world loves you. You are here to rock this world!

Sun quintile Neptune:
Your Career Message:
Be the light of compassion.

Your Hidden Talent:

You carry an "other worldly glow," an aura that envelops you, quietly permeating your surroundings and affecting those with your warmth. You are here to awaken your hidden talent that can inspire others with your visions of the way things should be; you are a beacon for those in need—the candle in the dark, the lighthouse on the shore, the welcoming smile to strangers passing by.

You are the soft-spoken black reverend who speaks of Jesus as a dark-skinned Palestinian Jew, who beseeches others to love the Arab child, the Christian child, the Hindu child, to love those of all faiths and those who have no faith. You are the tiny woman who sweeps a dying man off the streets of Calcutta, washes him, and holds him in her arms as he dies.

You hold these truths in your heart in whatever work you do. Your vivid imagination may bring you wealth, may aid you in building a business empire, but you will always be aware of the needs of others. As the owner of a pizza empire, you quietly pay the rent-for-life of a civil rights icon, or as a reclusive writer you found a charity that provides books for the world's children, or as a school custodian you anonymously pay the year's tab for the lunches of a needy child.

You allow others to be who they are because you see their inner light through a richly colored stained-glass window that touches your spiritual core. You can lose yourself in mystical and religious ceremonies, in an inspired work of art, or in the eyes of the helpless.

You have the ability to translate the vast creative images in your mind into the light of awareness, to be a beacon of compassion who will affect the lives of those in your all-encompassing embrace. They see you as you sweep by, but more than that, they feel you, causing them to turn their heads and wonder why they suddenly feel warmed by visions of sugar-plums and mermaids and fairy tales, and they smile.

Through the path you choose, you will be recognized for your compassionate contributions to your society; you are the gentle wave on a sun-kissed shore that washes over the hearts of others.

You open your window on the wold each morning with a smile. You know, as Zig Ziglar said, "A smile is your greatest social asset."

Sun quintile Pluto:
Your Career Message:
Be the light of resurrection.

Your Hidden Talent:

Others bemoan, "Oh, the weight of these splendid chains," however, you carry this mantle with ease. Your physical strength, regardless of your body's external condition, belies expectations. You are here to prove that, no matter how tired you are, you can draw from a hidden source to recharge your limitless internal battery and make fundamental change in the world. Tesla would be proud!

Quiet places, away from the hustle of the outside world, rejuvenate you. Working your body through yoga or working your mind through meditation require periods of isolation where your find and rejuvenate your inner strength.

Because you understand the laws that govern the hidden processes of life, your work this lifetime is to find the crack in those foundations, and then to resurrect that which is crumbling and ready for demolition and rebirth, psychologically or physically.

Your have the ability to translate your personal message to the world in almost Haiku-like poetry: concise, intense, and to the point. Your economy of words lends greater impact than the lengthy diatribes of others. It's like the grown son who, after his mother's lengthy warning about taking safety precautions on his foreign trip, responds simply "I'll be careful."

You have a subtle aura, an almost invisible cloak, that allows you to remain inconspicuous when you want to be. You can be in the middle of a room full of people, and someone will ask where you are. When you're pointed out, the comment is, "Oh, there you are. I didn't see you."

However, they will feel you. When you want to exercise your almost magical power to transform situations, you are a force to be reckoned with. Your intensity powers what you do and often your conversations seem to hypnotize others.

Sitting on boards that handle finances and large money transactions also fits your skill set. Whatever career you undertake, you have solutions to solve problems at deep fundamental levels.

You are the power not only behind the throne but on the throne in this lifetime. With almost magician-like talents, you transform circumstances through the use of your powerful will and your uncanny knowing of how things work. You are the example of one who overcomes the impossible.

⊙ **Q ASC** **Sun quintile Ascendant:**
Your Career Message:
Be there, be present.

Your Hidden Talent:
You have a talent to draw a crowd when you speak. Your enthusiastic presentation and boundless energy entertains people. Knowing how to say things and how to deliver a message with drama is your forte. You enliven discussions with your confident mannerisms and your zest for life. Your mission, if you choose it, is to be in the present, to light up and be noticed.

You are at heart a happy, outgoing person who sees the world in bright colors. Because you exude excitement and vitality, you can relate to people of all ages, and you are able to speak to them on their wavelengths. They appreciate your warmness and good sense of humor.

Because you are seen as an authority figure, you are here to be a spokesperson, to shine a light on your personal message. As a politician, teacher, actor, or parent, you put yourself into every moment of your day. And each day is a new day for you, a new day to interact and learn, to follow your curiosity wherever it leads you.

You start each day positively. Because you think positively, you draw positive situations and people to you, a positive catch 22. What you send out comes back to you. Scientists say the universe is "mind stuff," and your mind is stuffed with good thoughts and honorable intentions. Because people know you don't expect anything from them, because they know you give of yourself because that's who you are, they are willing to help you in response.

Your creative abilities may find expression in the theater and the arts. You could also shine in sports where again you would entertain the crowds. You recognize the need for a good education so that you can articulate the many thoughts that light up your curious mind. Whatever profession you choose, you will be the star; your presence and your words add sparkle to any performance.

You are the conversationalist par excellence; you love to talk and interact on a daily basis. You are here to prove that good intentions, a belief in your message, and a positive outlook can destine one for stardom.

You open your window on the world each morning with a smile. You know, as Zig Ziglar said, "A smile is your greatest social asset."

MERCURY SPEAKS TO THINKING AND COMMUNICATION

Mercury quintile Venus:
Your Career Message:
Wag your silver tongue.

Your Hidden Talent:
You are here to speak to issues of love, beauty, balance, harmony, and justice. Quite a mouthful! But you can do it because you have the silver tongue of a great orator.

You need a stage or a public podium from which to speak, or if you're more introverted, a den from where you can express your talent as the silver-penned writer. You draw from an internal dictionary that supports your flow of words. You have an elegance and grace that needs expression. Poetry is another talent where your elegant use of language naturally finds flower.

You don't ruffle feathers, but you do cast spells with your voice that can conjure up Love Potion Number 9 and charm the public. Perhaps your voice is your profession through music, commercials, and voice-overs. The combination of your melodic voice and your silver tongue mesmerizes an audience.

Your charm is an asset in public relations as well as business matters because you don't threaten others. You know how to compromise, to find that balance that allows others to accept what you have to say without sacrificing their own thoughts. Like Vulcan Mr. Spock's mind-meld ability, you seem to be able to convince others of your point of view.

Your talent is your creative mind combined with your charm. Although this is a soft-spoken talent, your voice carries great weight—sort of like those times when you were naughty and Mom just stood there, arms akimbo, calmly hovering over you like a protective but instructional angel, not saying a word . . . sort of mind-melding with you . . . and you knew you were in the proverbial hot water. She didn't have to say a word.

Think of a room full of noisy people arguing their point of view when suddenly the room quiets as a soft voice "overpowers" the cantankerous arguments at the town meeting or in the board room. Your voice quiets the fire-and-brimstone speaker; you bring the voice of reason, which soothes the most savage beast.

Your message places you in positions of leadership through gentle persuasion. You are the voice of justice, the mind-melder.

 **Mercury quintile Mars:**
Your Career Message:
Ruffle feathers.

Your Hidden Talent:

You know that expression: She can talk her way out of a paper bag? That begs the question as to how she ever got into that position in the first place. She's in there because of her curiosity, her search for information. That's you! Your talent is that you can lead others into the paper bag and then to lead them out once again with your MacGyver-like solutions.

Your early family may have threatened to paint a question mark on your forehead to warn others to flee as you approached. You are here to breathe fire into your continual search for information. Your insatiable mental curiosity drives a sharp mind, and you're fearless in your pursuit of knowledge.

Time to ruffle feathers but in a friendly way. Your natural ability to effortlessly communicate clearly puts others at ease and opens avenues to your success as a leader. Others see your ideas as useful, practical, and providing clever solutions, so they listen to you with open minds.

You're not afraid to reach out to others, to take that first step, because you have planned your actions in advance. You're not afraid to speak up when you see something amiss, and you don't miss much. You have the courage of your convictions. You feel that it is better to attempt to climb the mountain than to remain at the bottom and wish you had at least made an attempt.

You're a great tactician, knowing how to put things together to make them work. Chess, anyone? You're suited for many fields from engineering, military planning, and business to teaching, writing, and reporting. You're the fiery reporter who chases down every lead, the lawyer who devastates the opposition with your sharp informed rebuttals, the librarian who searches the dusty archives for that tiny bit of information you need to finish the thesis, and the writer who rolls around on the floor for days looking for that one word that accurately completes his thought. Think Flaubert.

As Ann Landers wrote, "The trouble with talking too fast is you may say something you haven't thought of yet." But that's just fine with you. You enjoy the challenge.

You have a facility with words that leads you willingly into the paper bag, which is your comfort zone because there you have the opportunity to use your talents to get out of it. You are here to own the paper bag factory.

☿ Q ♃

Mercury quintile Jupiter:
Your Career Message:
Ask questions.

Your Hidden Talent:

That almost invisible curlicue on your forehead is not a birthmark; it's a question mark. Your thirst for knowledge knows no bounds. Before the Internet you were surrounded by dictionaries, encyclopedias, maps, biographies, novels, and now you have added a computer and at least two iPads, one powering up to use when the first runs out of juice, so that you have access to your continual search for knowledge.

You're not preparing for a spot on *Jeopardy,* which tests your ability to remember facts, but you should use your mental talent to reach for a public platform from which your expertise can be used for the public good. Your breadth of knowledge must be shared with others through such venues as writing, teaching, philosophy, higher education, and through the courts of law.

Your curiosity may take you to foreign shores where you physically experience the cultures of those who live and think differently than you do. Your agile mind picks up foreign languages with ease; this increases your knowledge through the nuances of their speech patterns.

You view life optimistically and desire to lift others by elevating their minds to embrace the importance of education. You are an inspiring teacher and example for others. Your lifelong pursuit of knowledge is your joy in life attested to by the eclectic stack on books on the floor beside your bed, which never seems to diminish even though you read yourself to sleep each night. The 3:00 a.m. book fairies make special deliveries to your bedside each night.

You know the power of positive thinking because you live and breathe it. You realize that what you focus on, and the attitude you have towards life, dictates what comes back to you. That's not to say your life is all rich chocolate and rose-colored glasses, but you know what to do when life hands you a problem: explore the terrain, then reach for an intelligent solution.

Your optimistic attitude coupled with your breadth of knowledge and experience guides you to fields of power where your communication skills reign. You can be acknowledged as an example of someone who lifts and inspires others through the exploration of education. You have the power of the Word.

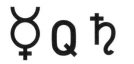 **Mercury quintile Saturn:**
Your Career Message:
Think inside the box.

Your Hidden Talent:
The World War II message "Loose lips sink ships" resonates within you.

You are the strong silent type. As a child no one knew what you were thinking; you probably didn't say much, keeping your thoughts to yourself. You were aware that words matter and what you say has consequences. You are here to show that an economy of words builds more lasting value than a dissertation.

You learned early that words are stone walls that enclose thoughts and keep them safe. You take umbrage with the old farmer in Robert Frost's poem "Mending Wall," who disagrees with his neighbor's postulation that "Something there is that doesn't love a wall . . ." You love walls, fences, boundaries, limits, rules, because they are your comfort zone. You thrive within them.

Your ideas are set in stone, but if enough provable new facts are unearthed, you will incorporate them into your well-ordered mind.

You can access facts easily because you have a good memory. You think things through, and you know how to plan and put plans into concrete results, because your thinking rests upon the proven research of the past. Combined with your organizational skills, many fields are open to you—education, science, research, politics, and architecture to name a few.

You develop a reputation for dependable, mature action. You say what you mean and mean what you say. Your word is your bond and you can be trusted to follow through on your contracts.

You learn by listening and studying and thinking, and then assembling those thoughts into lessons that you present as the teacher. This is the high school teacher you feared because she was too tough, but as an adult you have come to appreciate her now because she taught you so much; this is the politician who is ethical, the scientist who respects the rules of the past but will listen to new thoughts if they make sense.

You are here to be an example of one who thinks inside the box and lives by the rules and the written word. As a result you can be recognized in your community as a serious, trustworthy, and honorable person whose personal opinions and ideas have built stronger, more comfortable word boxes.

Mercury quintile Uranus:
Your Career Message:
Think outside the box.

Your Hidden Talent:

A touch of the genius, able to leap tall buildings in a single bound . . . oh, wait a minute, that's Superman. You are super*woman*, able to leap tall mental buildings. While everyone else is trying to figure out the problem by taking step one, step two, step three, you take two steps and make a quantum leap to the thousandth step. Everyone blinks and asks: Who are you? How did you get to that conclusion? A quick change in the phone booth and you look like everyone else. However . . .

. . . your intuitive leaps are based on the initial facts. Your genius lies in putting those facts together and, like greased lightning, finding the solution. You are here to develop this talent.

Because you are curious and alert and knowledgeable about so many eclectic subjects, inspiration hits like a thunder bolt. Along with a touch of your genius, you find the answers.

You need the freedom to think in you own unique manner. You belong in a think tank or a business where you have free reign to explore many unusual concepts that others poo-poo or haven't even thought of yet.

Your mind is so active that you may find it hard to sleep because ideas keep popping in to visit in those wee hours. You definitely need a notebook and pen by your bedside, even if you have to scribble messages in the dark so as not to disturb your bedmate. The problem may be in deciphering those scratchings in the morning, but you'll figure it out because . . . well . . . because you are intuitive!

You easily inspire those around you who are intellectually curious. You can spark others' inventive tendencies in the laboratory, the classroom, in technology, in ecology, in the literary field. You are a progressive thinker who can blaze new trails throughout your life. You also understand the importance of sharing your ideas with the world, for the betterment of society as a whole.

You can be recognized in this lifetime for your achievements, which will be seen as unique and different, somewhat strange. But hey, that's a compliment as far as you're concerned. The greatest insult, as far as you're concerned, is that you think like everyone else. No one will ever accuse you of that!

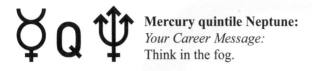

Mercury quintile Neptune:
Your Career Message:
Think in the fog.

Your Hidden Talent:
You have the talent to consciously interpret those images that are beyond the five senses. You came into this world on "little cat's paws" to see into the fog. In other words, you are clairvoyant. A psychic senses and reacts to the unseen field around her; it's an emotional connection. A clairvoyant like you consciously interprets the subtle fields; it's an intellectual connection. Psychics feel; you see.

This connection between your intuitive insight and your vast imagination is the reason that you often anticipate the emotional reactions of others. In this manner you are able to overcome obstacles that others might not foresee.

Some might think you a witchy woman, like one of the three witches in Shakespeare's *Macbeth*, able to prophesy the future. However, you view your ability as simple reasoning . . . a sort of mental telepathy where you sense the thoughts of others before they are openly expressed. You are here to develop this talent before the public.

Images and insights pop into your mind. You never know when this will happen, so you should always have a pen and small notebook handy in which to record those thoughts—in your pocket while you take a walk, beside your favorite easy chair, at work, in a restaurant where, of course, you can always scribble on a napkin.

Your dreams are a source of inspiration as well. Record your dreams; when you wake in the morning, remain still and let your most recent dream come to the surface. Many inventions and creative inspirations arise here.

You genuinely want to help others; you are sympathetic to the foibles of others and do not judge them. You care, and because you do, people feel comfortable in your presence. They sense your compassion and know they are safe with you. They know you are not overly concerned with the material world but are guided by spiritual values. Others see you through this lens.

Your talent lies in being able to give a voice to your great imagination through the arts, such as writing and photography, education, medicine, and social programs. You can inspire others through your accomplishments. You can be recognized in your lifetimes as a leader in your particular field, one whose compassion and vast creative vision deserve recognition.

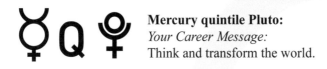

Mercury quintile Pluto:
Your Career Message:
Think and transform the world.

Your Hidden Talent:

Remember the childhood game of blind man's bluff where one person is blindfolded and cannot see but attempts to touch other players? You always won that game because you have x-ray vision. The Shaolin priest may walk through walls, but you see through walls. You are here to give voice to that which lies hidden within.

You have an intellect that can penetrate the most obtrusive subjects and complicated problems and easily make sense of them. Able to dig to the root of a situation, you find answers.

You are the detective of the zodiac, using your mental agility and curiosity to think things through to the end. Your subject can run but can't hide because you never give up the search.

An old African proverb states "walk softly but carry a big stick." You walk softly but carry an intense intellect that believes the mind is mightier than the sword. You can wield that sword from your position at the head of such institutions as a financial entity, a law enforcement agency, an alphabetical security agency, a think tank, through psychology and research, or through the escapades of a fictional crime fighter.

Your keen intellect uncovers what others think is hidden. Your psychic ability, almost like black magic, reveals the hidden workings behind the physical world. You are unafraid to plumb the depths in order to reveal and transform the world around you. This ability translates into your conversations with people who begin to sense you know what they're thinking. They may feel naked under your gaze as your eyes focus in on them.

You are able to focus your mind like a laser. Your penetrating insights astound others. Maybe it's those eyes that seem to hypnotize. You have the look of a witchy woman, sensual and mysterious.

Needless to say, you are intense. Your standing in the world, how you are viewed, and your career goals are built upon your investigative talents and your ability to convey these ideas into powerful and transformative directives. You can be recognized in your lifetime for your ability to bring about fundamental change through the power of your words and your mind.

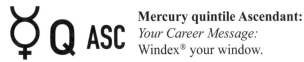

Mercury quintile Ascendant:
Your Career Message:
Windex® your window.

Your Hidden Talent:

"Curiouser and curiouser!" cried Alice. "Now I'm opening out like the largest telescope that ever was!" That's you! You have an insatiable curiosity that never stops mentally collecting and disseminating information. All things being equal—as if they ever are—you should set up an information booth and charge for your services. Your hidden talent is your access to an encyclopedic amount of facts and your ability to get those facts across to others in a friendly, conversational manner.

You may have been surrounded by books as a child, but more likely your library is the outdoors where you converse with "the baker, the butcher, and the candlestick maker" as well as exploring the environment from the mightiest conifers housing owls down to the intricate beauty of the mosses and their nematode inhabitants. No source of information is too far out for your curious mind.

You're aware of body language, those subtleties that we all express and are not aware of because we don't see ourselves from the outside. Does the hitch of the brow show disdain—the biting of the lower lip show insecurity—the crossing of the arms shut out people? You observe these nuances.

You are a clever and witty conversationalist because you never run out of things to talk about. Because your observations of and encounters with people are more intellectual, your observations are not clouded by emotion. You learn something every day and from every conversation and encounter.

Your realize that even punctuation can change the meaning of a written message. Note the wandering commas from Lynne Truss's book, *Eats, Shoots and Leaves*:

A woman, without her man, is nothing.

A woman, without her, man is nothing.

You belong in the field of communications: teaching, writing, mediating, scientific research. You are here to be the celestial postman who collects and disseminates data, then translates that information into exciting new ideas that provide a new look at the world through a sparkling clean window. Stock up on Windex®.

VENUS SPEAKS TO LOVE, BEAUTY, AND JUSTICE

♀ Q ♂ **Venus quintile Mars:**
Your Career Message:
Love equality.

Your Hidden Talent:
Men are from Mars; women are from Venus. So wrote John Gray in his popular 1992 book of the same title. On the cover, the word men was mentioned first in bold black text; the word woman followed in flowery pink smaller text, highlighting the differences between the sexes. The theme: men offer a straightforward solution; women want to talk about it.

Of course women want to talk about it! By talking, you create the opportunity to look at given solutions from different points of view in order to find the balance between the two. The goal: a just settlement.

Your hidden talent is your need for peace, which you apply to relationships where you act as an arbitrator, counselor, or diplomat. You are the peacekeeper reaching for common ground. You find yourself in the limelight when things get difficult because others instinctively look to you to settle disputes.

Your likability and charming manner with both sexes engages others because of your non-threatening nature. You embody that open non-judgmental acceptance that sets people at ease. You would excel in the courtroom and the halls of government because you truly believe in equality and justice.

There is a physical grace that accompanies your talent—"She walks in beauty" sort of thing. The energy that drives you can manifest in yoga, dance, the joy of gliding through a field of buttercups; you are beauty in motion.

Your artistic talent may find a home in professions that provide beauty such as interior design, landscaping, fashion, beauty products and makeovers, where you create a setting and a mind-set that encourages self-esteem. A beautiful garden, a lovely home, the perfect hairstyle and makeup lifts the spirits and in turn inspires a feeling of balance and well-being.

Whether it's diplomacy that prevents wars, beauty makeovers for women in depressed circumstances that boosts their self-esteem, or justice for all, use your talents to lift spirits and increase self-confidence through beauty and balance. From a public platform, you are here to fight for equality so the book titles in the future will display the same size font.

♀ Q ♃ **Venus quintile Jupiter**
Your Career Message:
Spread the love.

Your Hidden Talent:
"Sugar and spice and everything nice; that's what little girls are made of." This old nursery rhyme applies to you. Your talent is sharing your joy.

You have a loving and generous nature, and your cheerful attitude lifts the spirits of those you meet. You welcome the world with open arms, spreading joy as you interact with others. If thoughts are things, as science tell us, than you will bring good things into your life (you do like nice things) as well as into the lives of others.

Because of your sympathetic nature, you're always willing to listen to the problems of others. You know the right things to say to ease their discomforts. You articulate the goodness you find in life with grace. You would make a fine teacher whose students would be lifted by your optimism and personal view of life, a great gift for those who need to see life as the sparkling glass bubbling over.

You should be visible in your career because your warm personality will endear you to your audience. This coupled with your fine sense of design can bring you success. You also have a good business sense when it comes to all things creative. You might find you are talented in remodeling and decorating homes and businesses. You could follow in the footsteps of Joanna Gaines of the HGTV show, *Fixer Upper*.

Your leadership abilities may involve education where you have access to a vast audience. Your subjects will not be deep and dark; on the contrary they will lift others through expanding their reach into that big wide world out there in which they can grow and find their happy spot.

You have the sweet harmony of words, which could lead you to the travel industry as a guide where you would be more successful than most. You could even write about your experiences, another avenue for your creativity. Articles and short stories are more likely to your taste; you do like comfort time.

You learn through tasting, touching, smelling, and feeling life's experiences on a broad scale. You career should involve using these sensual delights to help others. You are still the little girl in the candy store, eyes wide, twinkling with delight!

Venus quintile Saturn:
Your Career Message:
Make love visible.

Your Hidden Talent:

The farmer at the end of Robert Frost's poem "Mending Wall," believes "Good fences make good neighbors." You would agree; you love fences. You understand that walls and fences are necessary in life. Words are fences that enclose our ideas. Skin is a wall that contains the bones and organs in our bodies. Rules and boundaries are part of your creative thought process.

You are here to use your talent to build something visible for the world to see. You don't clutter your expression with unnecessary elements; you get right to the bones of the matter. Your love of form and clean lines informs everything you do.

You structure your love, contain it within perimeters that you feel will endure. As an expression of your desire to give concrete expression to your considerable artistic tendencies, you may find an outlet for your talent through sculpture, an enduring art form, or through the collection of fine pieces of art that reflect quality. You look for the timelessness in your collection. You feel that less reveals more of the beauty. As the musician Sting said, "Music is the silence between the notes."

You may find expression through serious and thoughtful writings or by teaching the rules and values necessary in business and government, or by working for legislation that embodies the codes of conduct that affect a civilized society.

As the leader of a company, you would apply your serious approach to life to all that you do. You are willing to work as hard as those over whom you preside. You would treat your employees like a strict parent who knows that discipline is a form of love. Follow the rules, do your job with a positive attitude, and you will be reward in equal measure.

You could be a respected mediator who cuts through the confusion and discord between opposing parties and comes to a clean-cut decision that is fair to both sides.

You make your mark in this world through the concrete expression of your artistry. You can be recognized as someone whose creative talent is backed up by honesty, integrity, and steadfastness. You are here to prove that love can be made visible.

Venus quintile Uranus:
Your Career Message:
Love differences.

Your Hidden Talent:
You sparkle aplenty! Like the stars in the firmament, you shine just because that's what you do. You're in love with the honeymoon of love, that period when everything is new and exciting and experimental because it allows you the freedom to express yourself in unusual and inventive ways.

You don't discriminate by shining on only a few. You gather everyone in your starlit embrace, entertaining and exciting them with your warmth and understanding. This innate talent primes you for success in many fields. Perhaps it's those deep dimples and cherubic smile that gets them.

You do add excitement to any gathering. It's your charming romantic nature that endears you to others. Plus, you are willing to compromise, to a point, as long as it doesn't infringe upon your need for independence and freedom in your relationships. You allow others the freedom to be themselves; your progressive attitude allows for surprise and innovation. You are indeed the life of the party!

The originality you bring to your creative talents in the fields of art and music can manifest in unusual forms of expression, often involving technical aspects. You may have an interest in a profession in television, the Internet, microchips and the computer, gaming, any new-age expression of your abilities interest you. You can make your money and your mark professionally through these markets. Plus, you have many friends who will connect you to those who will aid you in your career goals.

You may be noted for a new invention, an unusual approach to the way you handle your business ventures. Because you are always aware of the goals of others, you find ways to bring them into your fold, thus creating a cooperative effort.

You are the charming eccentric Willy Wonka who provides the golden ticket to the delicious wonders of the world of chocolate, opening your business doors to those who wish to have the opportunity to share in what you have created.

On the romantic side note, you've been known to tuck a romantic poem along with a dark-chocolate bonbon beneath your lover's pillow to remind your partner that the love fairy has visited. You have the opportunity to leave your chocolate-smudged fingerprints on the world's face. Yum!

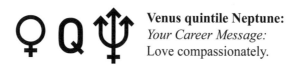

Venus quintile Neptune:
Your Career Message:
Love compassionately.

Your Hidden Talent:
There's an element of the savior in you who can, on the one hand, romanticize love in sweet verse or, on the other hand, can sweep in to save those in need. The question is into what category do you fall? Were you reading fairy tales as a child or sharing your allowance with a hungry classmate?

Your compassion and need to balance the books stretches across the spectrum from the ivory tower of idealized love exemplified by one of the finest lyric poets of the English romantics to the practical love demonstrated by one of "the most trusted financial wizards" of the twentieth century who, unbeknownst to the public was not a wise old man but an attractive twenty-nine-year- old woman, who switched her major from English literature to economics after the Stock Market Crash of 1929.

Your talent is your ability to calm the troubled waters and bestow a peaceful hand over the storms that lie in the hearts of the troubled. You are here to exercise your emotional empathy to soothe souls and solve problems.

You may be the romantic poet whose imagination taps into pools of creative richness, sharing a world of idealized romance. Or you may find a niche in the healing arts such as massage, tai chi, meditation, or sacred circle dancing. Or you could find solace in your church, be it an ancient stone cathedral whose stained glass light casts rainbows of promise over your kneeling body or in the enchanted forests where light pools on the soft pine carpet beneath the boughs of nature's magnificent church built of bark and greenery.

And then again you may find your talent suited to social services that uplift those who are suffering economically. Love draws you to those who need you.

You do need a sanctuary where you can periodically escape from the unsettling psychic interferences of the everyday world. Your dreams are a source of wisdom. Many solutions, inventions, and creative inspirations have awakened in that nebulous world.

You are here to develop your talent, which is your spiritual contribution to the work that you do, the care you take in handling others, the beauty you create, and the uplifting messages that soothe those to whom you speak and with whom you interact.

Venus quintile Pluto:
Your Career Message:
Love passionately.

Your Hidden Talent:

Your talent is the intensity with which you approach life. You cannot love half way. In fact, it is someone like you who wrote the marriage vow, "'til death do us part." Those are not just words to you; they are words to live by. You are here to express your deep commitment to those causes that will bring about fundamental change in relationships and in the resources needed to sustain a balanced register.

There is a mystery about you, a magnetic quality, a charisma that draws people to you . . . sort of the bad girl/bad boy persona. Others know you are deep, that you hold secrets and contain mysteries, and this only adds to your allure.

All your relationships are intense whether they are personal, social, or business related. You know of no other way to interact with others. Words matter; when you give your word, you stand by it and expect others to do the same.

If applied to your artistic side, this intensity manifests dramatically in music or art where your creative side expresses the depth of your feelings. Your canvas or musical composition or performance stirs fundamental desires in the publics' emotions that draw them inward to examine their own inner worlds. You are the magician who reveals inner landscapes through your art.

You do have an uncanny sense that accurately perceives the intentions of others, so your profession may involve detection on some level. You would make a fine therapist, able to psychically tune in to the root motivations of patients without traveling down side roads that lead nowhere.

Because money is part of gaining what we desire, finances may be one avenue of success for you. You understand that resources are fundamental to support society, therefore, your profession may involve uncovering fraud in financial or public institutions. You will expose the offenders!

You attract financial support when you need it. You are comfortable working with wealthy people and with powerful institutions. Your quiet charm inspires confidence so that you are able to convince plutocrats to use their considerable resources to transform the lives of others. You are here to use your powerful magic to rebuild crumbling relationships and power structures.

♀ Q ASC
Venus quintile Ascendant:
Your Career Message:
Love your view.

Your Hidden Talent:
You open your eyes every day and smell the flowers. You look through a window colored with peace, beauty, and harmony.

Your talent is your ability to express your ideas with an inborn grace and gentility; this goes a long way to soothing disputes and maintaining friendly contacts. You will bend considerably to understand opposing points of view because peace is essential to your physical and mental well-being.

Balance is so important that you may find yourself straightening picture frames, making sure your shoe lacings hang evenly, that the objects on your desk are aligned perfectly, and that can of peas on the supermarket floor is replaced on the shelf, label facing front.

You speak in a refined manner because of your love of language. You dislike coarse or foul language, seeing it as a lack of manners. Your refined tastes are also displayed in the selection of your wardrobe, your line of cosmetics, the elegant fragrances you choose. You may channel your creative ability into writing, music, art, interior decorating, and related businesses.

If you write, it is from a platform where you speak personally and inclusively to the reader. As a speaker you are aware of your audience, focusing in on anyone who seems uneasy, then setting about to include that person in your talk. At a party, you notice the person who seems neglected and alone, and you will engage her in friendly conversation so she will feel included.

You feel it's important to have friendly contact with those people you interact with on a daily basis.

You have a gentleness that radiates out to those around you. Beauty and color is important in your life. You love nice things and surround yourself with those things at work and in your home which may be your workplace. This type of environment provides you with comfort and happiness.

Diplomacy and charm are the talents you possess and should employ to bring balance, beauty, and harmony into your daily life. You have an innate joy and happiness, a lighthearted spirit, that delights your friends and is an asset to any groups to which you belong. Use you voice to sell those fabled rose-colored glasses because you prove they do work.

MARS SPEAKS TO THE ACTION PRINCIPLE

♂ Q ♃

Mars quintile Jupiter:
Your Career Message:
Reach beyond your grasp.

Your Hidden Talent:
When people tell you to "go fly a kite," meaning "go away, you're bothering me," you're out the door searching for the nearest beach or open field praying for a good wind. Perhaps in more current vernacular the expression is "go fly a drone." At any rate . . .

. . . pity those poor people because they will never know what it means to reach for the heights. Your talent is that you will never stop reaching. That high jump record, you'll strive to clear it one inch higher; that marathon winning time, you'll finish it one minute faster; that lecture, you'll have them standing on their feet asking for more! You are here to prove that "your reach should exceed your grasp."

You desire both physical and intellectual competition. You can be successful because you put so much energy into your efforts, and you know what you are talking about. You base your information on knowledge you have accumulated as the result of your continual intellectual drive.

You need to use your flair for presentation and your confidence in your knowledge because it leads to victory. Your missionary zeal includes the less fortunate in your efforts, and you will defend those who don't know how to speak for themselves. Your generous spirit and courage in speaking your convictions draws people to you.

You are ambitious in a positive way. You instinctively know that the secret to success is timing and you have a keen sense of timing. You should be at the top as the inspired leader of any enterprise you choose. You would be effective as the head of a business, a teacher in a university, an ethical politician, a lawyer defending the rights of less privileged, or in the vast reaches of today's media.

You have a powerful voice, an optimistic message, that will gain you a following. People know they can trust that you will do the right thing, that you have their best interests in mind.

You can be recognized for using these considerable skills in the work you choose to do. You are here to make a difference from a position of power, and to be seen and remembered as the one who reached for and grasped the gold ring.

♂ Q ♄ **Mars quintile Saturn:**
Your Career Message:
Look before you leap.

Your Hidden Talent:
Your talent is your patience and endurance. You will go the extra mile. Recognize that your willingness to put in the time to achieve your goals, and your disciplined approach to your work can lead to great achievements built on solid bedrock, like the engineer who blueprinted the Great Wall of China or the overseer for the construction of the great cathedrals of Europe, or the founder of great documents that laid out the rules to protect society.

You believe in rules because they order a life that is safe within predictable walls. With rules, you can depend upon the smooth running of the world you live in.

You don't waste time. In fact, you may still remember that anonymous poem forced upon you by an old high school teacher: I have only just a minute, only sixty seconds in it . . . give a count if I abuse it . . . just a tiny little minute, but eternity is in it.

Your plans are practical, taking into account all the possible contingencies so that your strategy is almost always a winning one because you stick to your well-thought-out plan. You have the mind of a military tactician or chess champion.

You have the courage to overcome fears because you base your efforts on the tried and true experiences of the past. Once you decide upon a project, you will continue on that path forever, if necessary, because you have based your knowledge on facts. And on your considerable patience.

You are self-disciplined and will accomplish whatever you choose to do. And you can convince others because, in any debate, you can back up your statements. The details never escape you.

You believe "success is ten percent inspiration and ninety percent perspiration." As the leader of any enterprise or business, you are respected for your preparedness and expect the same from others. You are not all warm and fuzzy; rather you are all business, often preferring to work alone or at the top of the hill where you can concentrate uninterrupted; therefore you are often seen as a lone fighter.

Your job is to be recognized by the public as a trusted figure who will fight for a safe and well-ordered society supported by rules that will endure. Hi-ho, Silver.

Mars quintile Uranus:
Your Career Message:
Take a leap.

Your Hidden Talent:
You are here to test the limits. Free falling from the sky, shot from a cannon, crossing the Grand Canyon on a tightrope, whatever it takes to pump up the adrenaline is hiding in your wheelhouse. You are ready for action; actually you thrive on it. Dynamic and impulsive, you want to revel in challenges, and once that challenge is accomplished, you're ready for the next adventure.

Your talent is the courage to forge forward . . . rules do not apply. You need to challenge traditional ideas if they don't make sense and don't apply anymore. Free the rebel lurking inside you to enthusiastically promote the thrill of adventure and jump-start the progressive ideas that will help others.

In your personal life, you like experimentation and excitement and variety. Your unconventional attitude towards relationships won't tolerate possessive family, partners, or friends. Most likely you have a wide circle of eclectic friends because they stimulate the variety you seek.

You need room in your career to use your intellectual curiosity and original ideas. You're always ready to move forward with a new thought and you find it hard to work with people who are too slow to accept your unique approach, although you have the ability to present your point of view persuasively. You never seem at a loss for words.

Your mind is lightning quick; your flashes of intuition can lead to startling innovative techniques that challenge and possibly change traditional methods.

The world is your laboratory, and nothing escapes your interest. You like to know how things work, so the scientific, mechanical, and technical fields are open for your keen exploration. Since the sky's the limit, you may find the field of aviation is right up your flight plan.

Your position in society will be unique. You can be recognized as the genius inventor, the forward thinker, the leader who will never give up, and who will challenge the failing doctrines of the past. You are here to be decisive and daring, to leave most people in a trail of physical and intellectual dust wondering how they will ever keep up with you but marveling at the excitement and adventurous spirit you stir within their breasts.

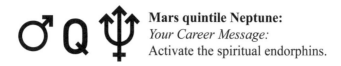 **Mars quintile Neptune:**
Your Career Message:
Activate the spiritual endorphins.

Your Hidden Talent:
Sign up for a respite in a flotation chamber. Floating in salt water where the outside world is shut out and you let go of all sensory perceptions, you reach deep levels of tranquility and heightened awareness. Muscles relax, heart rate slows, and those happy endorphins are released into your body.

Given your sensitivity to the harshness of the world, on doctor's advice this could be great therapy for you. Loosened from the bonds of earth, you enter a spiritual world where your imagination floats freely, where you are able to reach into your dream world.

The healing effects of periodic temporary escapes from the harsher realities of society cannot be overstated. Once replenished, you are here to work for those less fortunate because you practice your faith in the real world.

You are a healer. In whatever profession you choose, you use your touch to serve the greater good. Medicine in its various forms benefits from your presence because of your healing aura. Your psychic abilities and sensitivity work hand-in-hand with your compassionate drive to serve others.

You are the strategist whose natural instincts aid you in avoiding barriers that would prevent you from achieving your goals. You can work behind the scenes, anonymously if necessary, to maneuver the chess pieces to the final checkmate. Your natural instincts give you an advantage in achieving victory.

Your creative imagination is boundless. You may be drawn to professions that require fluid physical activity such as dance, yoga, and other performing arts. You also have the ability to tell stories that draw upon the fantasies of others, the romantic side that whisks them away into a more mystical world. You sense what others need and you are here to develop that creative ability for a glimpse into ethereal worlds.

Your talent lies in taking a leadership role in your profession where you represent a spiritual "warrior" standing for those in society who need help, and an inspiration for those who yearn to touch the beauty of an unfettered imagination. You may do this in a business venture, as an effective counselor, or in the arts but, whichever path you choose, you are here to apply your considerable talent to stimulating the conscience of society.

Mars quintile Pluto:
Your Career Message:
Sharpen your shovels.

Your Hidden Talent:
Keep your shovels sharp and at hand. You are here as a digger into underlying causes—which brings to mind memories of the 1944 radio show *The Life of Riley,* featuring Digger O'Dell, the Friendly Undertaker. You're not here to "go shoveling off" but rather to take spade in hand and get to the bottom of things.

Your talent is your powerful, driving force that will overcome unbelievable odds. With an endless supply of energy, you search for truths that will transform the world as you know it. You can expose the naked truth.

You are the dogged detective aware of the hidden motivations of others. If you are on the trail, they might as well give up now and save everyone the trouble, because your X-ray instinct picks up on the most subtle clues. You know human behavior and all its frailties and will solve the puzzle with dispatch. You know it's not always "the butler who did it."

You are here to take courageous action in the face of danger. You instinctively know how to overcome the odds and defeat the enemy. You have an inner strength that would serve you well in combat, endurance sports, and any activities that require physical endurance. You don't do things half way; you do things all the way and beyond expectations.

You may dig into the minds of others as a therapist, into the world of finance, or into the political shenanigans of those in power. Your role as a public crusader or as an activist to save the planet from destructive forces can make a mark in society. You should actively pursue fundamental change in systems that are corrupt and failing in their responsibilities.

Use your determination to find ways to take charge, to lead the army and battle the forces that would try to control the will and resources of others. At times, these battles may take the form of a knock-down, drag out verbal debate. You can be a formidable opponent.

In your professional role, you are here to be recognized as a defender of the resources that ensure the well-being of the community and the world, with a little pugilistic fervor thrown in at times as well.

♂ Q ASC

Mars quintile Ascendant:
Your Career Message:
Sharpen your vision.

Your Hidden Talent:

You rush every morning to open your window on the world. You're up at the crack of dawn and ready to go. No more beating around the bush . . . you are here to trek through the landscape to get to your goal.

Your talent is that you get to the point quickly. Not one to dance around a conversation, you are frank and direct, and you say what you think with enthusiasm. Your words are full of energy and passion; you do make noise so there's no question that you will be heard. Most of the time you manage to do this in ways that evoke cooperation from others.

You are mentally and physically active, which is an outlet for your abundant energy. The first one to start the conversation or to lead the hike, you remain alert. Your physical agility may encourage athletic activity.

You are a hard worker at whatever you do, constantly coming up with new and creative ideas that will fix things. You should let others know that you can do the job. If you work for a company, you increase the output and stimulate positive competition with co-workers; if you run your own business, you work tirelessly to accomplish more than your competitors. You can inspire respect because you are willing to take on responsibility in whatever job you are assigned. Your enthusiasm is contagious.

You should be involved in the activity of life around you. Not much escapes your notice, which would serve you well as a reporter, a writer, someone involved in the communications media where your investigative skills are recognized. You see and immerse yourself in the vitality of daily life.

Your desire is to rise to the top where you can lead the pack in your chosen field. You see the world through a natural platform of competition. You are here to learn to use your boundless energy through your innate talent to achieve your goals. You have creative ideas, and that teamed with your boundless enthusiasm will aid you in achieving what it is that you seek, placing you in a position of leadership where you can inspire others to achieve their goals as well.

"Having someone who listens is a great gift, but to be truly heard is a treasure." You agree with Tatjana Urbic. You will be heard.

JUPITER SPEAKS TO GROWTH, OPTIMISM, AND KNOWLEDGE

♃ Q ♄ **Jupiter quintile Saturn:**
Your Career Message:
Knowledge builds history.

Your Hidden Talent:
Your hidden talent is your ability to translate your innate knowledge into a lasting structure. Knowledge is the keystone of your life because it supports the efforts you put into any endeavors you undertake. You are here to concretize what you know.

You have a big appetite for answers. When you are asked a question you don't know the answer to, immediately out comes the smartphone or iPad, or you dig into your vast store of books or take a trip into the bowels of the local library. You store away both tidbits and vast volumes and tuck them into your rather badly wrinkled brain. That's a compliment. Every time you learn something knew, you earn another wrinkle in your mental library.

You are an excellent planner because you can see the big picture as well as the structure that lies beneath. This talent enables you to complete big tasks.

You are willing to work hard. By employing practical guidelines in your climb to the top, you can succeed. You also adhere to ethical standards. You see to it that the job is handled professionally and that you live up to your high standards along the way, treating others with the respect you expect in return.

You can be successful because you operate between cautious planning and optimistic thinking. Your success is built upon your keen sense of timing. You know better than to plant healthy seeds in an arid desert in the middle of the summer.

Put your talent to good use. You can reign from a position of power in a number of fields—architecture, the law, education, foreign or public service, politics, writing—any career where your vast knowledge and forward thinking inspires others. People believe and trust that you can do what you say you can do. And that, as the say, you can take to the bank.

Your power comes from your concern for the well-tested laws that protect society but at the same time allow for progressive growth. You understand that society grows with the free expression of diversity. You are here to prove that from the top of the foundations you build, you can see across continents.

♃ Q ♅
Jupiter quintile Uranus:
Your Career Message:
Expand exponentially.

Your Hidden Talent:

Requesting a copy of the Declaration of Independence for your fifth birthday certainly startled your family. The fact that you then proceeded to read the entire document made them sit up and take notice that they had an unusual child. That's when the knowledge bug bit you.

Don't stop now. Don't dismiss that childhood pleasure. Your talent is your thirst for knowledge and your keen insights that will lead you on the path to progressive thinking. You need to look into the future for what the possibilities can be. You've always been curious, finding joy in exploring cultures beyond your own, where you can reach beyond traditional thought and explore worlds heretofore unknown.

Use that insatiable curiosity to tap into the public consciousness. You possess what others consider the gift of prophecy; however, it's based upon the enormous amount of knowledge that you have accumulated, and then, when needed, you make quantum leaps of logic to that eureka moment of discovery. While everyone else is going A—B—C—D . . . you have gone A—B—Z! Others are looking around asking, "Where did you go? How did you get to that conclusion?" You think it's obvious because your intuitive leaps are based upon logic.

You may find international travel a means by which you learn about how the world lives and thinks or you may be an armchair traveler surrounded by books, maps, iPads, computers, and a world globe. Whatever source of information is available, you will be sure you have access to it.

You are optimistic about the future and all its possibilities. Your positive attitude draws people to you. You are an exciting presence, able to talk on most any subject while offering new insights that stimulate people into thinking about their possibilities.

Your lightning-quick mind is always ready for an adventure into the world of discovery. Your public reputation in your chosen profession—religion, philosophy, science, the law, writing, teaching, the arts, politics, space exploration, or metaphysics—can lend credence to your visions of the future. You are here to use your creative mind to explore beyond the norm, to satisfy your bottomless yearning to know. You are meant to excite and motivate others to expand and discover their own worlds.

♃ Q ♆ Jupiter quintile Neptune:
Your Career Message:
Awaken the angels.

Your Hidden Talent:
You are a daydreamer with a boundless imagination. You are here to give voice to other worlds beyond the sight of most. Your expansive imagination lends itself to creative writing, music, and spiritual practices where you give form to what others cannot envision. Art is in your soul.

Believing that the best in people can manifest in this world, you're an idealist who wants to make a difference, to use your influence to promote humanitarian agendas that ease the suffering of the most vulnerable in society. You reach out into the community through messages of compassion to touch the consciousness of the public to enlist support for your causes.

You can find a number of avenues to travel to attain your goals . . . through the political streets, the social landscapes, the religious and philosophical halls, and into the mystical realms of literature. You have faith that your voice will call to the moral fiber of those who will listen, and it will awaken their better angels.

Your creative imagination coupled with your emotions guides you through life. Your psychic, almost mystical power, is evident in your communication skills. You are a sensitive, picking up the motivations that drive people. Perhaps, at a fair, you dressed as a fortuneteller—head scarf, hoop earrings, and with a crystal ball—to raise money for your local charity or school, not even aware that people left your tent shaking their head at your accurate insight.

Your dreams are a source of creativity, the place you visit each night that's filled with fairies and fantasy, where you are freed from the restraints of the physical world, where you can imagine one hundred impossible things before breakfast.

You should record your dreams each morning, and browse through that diary each night before you fall asleep. Without the untold ideas, mystical and fanciful literature, and musical inspiration that was birthed in this secret, quiet place, the world would be much poorer.

Through your career choice, you are meant to give voice to your personal creative talents, to share your inspirational messages with the public so that their lives will be richer. Your ad in the classified: Dreamers may apply.

♃ Q ♇ Jupiter quintile Pluto:
Your Career Message:
Knowledge is power.

Your Hidden Talent:

You have an enormously powerful voice that is backed by knowledge. Because of this, you can affect far-reaching changes in this world. You understand what is hidden beneath surfaces and you have the faith to make those fundamental changes for the benefit of all.

Your curious mind investigates all the possibilities that are normally hidden from the understanding of others; you see beneath the surface at the underpinnings of human emotional needs. You understand the necessity to protect the resources that support us all, and you give a powerful voice to this understanding.

You have a compelling desire to understand large problems and to find positive solutions, and you have the philosophical strength to carry on against all odds. You speak eloquently and intensely about the need to tear down old worn-out institutions and modes of thought and rebuild from the ground up. At times, in the midst of intense philosophical debates, even your silence speaks volumes. You are here to work tirelessly from a public platform to achieve these goals.

You may contribute your own considerable resources both mentally and physically, through ideas and wealth, to achieve the transformation of that which has outlived its usefulness and has become an oppressive burden upon the world. Controlling financial and social institutions and governments, Big Brother and Doublethink, have no place in your world.

Because justice and the proper use of power is an issue in your life, you may find the halls of justice and the law as your pulpit. You could do as well in managing big business, or in the healing arts, any field that brings about positive transformation and regeneration.

Your hidden talent is your powerful voice, which is backed up by enormous amounts of research and knowledge. You have the faith and vision to reach out more globally to effect positive change in the world. You understand death and resurrection; you see it as a positive and necessary part of life. Through your career, you seek those elements in society that are decaying and see to it that they cross the River Styx and pay their fee to Charon, the ferryman, thus enriching this world.

♃ Q ASC

Jupiter quintile Ascendant:
Your Career Message:
Open your windows wide.

Your Hidden Talent:
Each day holds promise. Your gift to the world is the positive enthusiasm with which you welcome the morning. Your window on the world is wide open as you cheerfully anticipate what you have to do and where you have to go.

You greet each person with a smile and a positive message. Because you are generous towards others, you find support in return. You genuinely enjoy engaging in conversations with people, exchanging ideas, and offering them a daily dose of your cheer.

Decoratively framed on your inner walls are the paraphrased words that reflect *your hidden talent:* "As ye think positively, so shall ye be happy" and "for every positive action, there is an equal and opposite positive reaction."

People respect your considerable knowledge and the fact that you know what you're talking about. You constantly seek to expand your understanding of life. You are interested in many subjects and, in your quest to know, you have learned that listening is just as important as talking. You are a welcome presence at any business or social meeting, party, or accidental meeting in aisle five in the grocery store.

You understand that opening your window to other cultures to learn about how they think and live expands your view of the world and makes you a better person. You may find foreign travel a necessary part of your lifestyle because you want to "be there" to live and feel and discuss other lifestyles and beliefs.

You promote education as a broadening influence and as the key to a successful life, the path to a hopeful future where people can believe in themselves and look forward with confidence to a brighter future. You're always ready to help others in their pursuit of furthering themselves. Your optimistic message encourages others to have faith that life will turn out well if they think positively.

You are here to speak from a public platform with the authority of the well-informed and to be recognized for your verbal skills and broad knowledge of the world in the fields of communication such as teaching, writing, philosophical and religious arenas, and other media outlets. Others can benefit from your open embrace of world cultures and their differences.

SATURN SPEAKS TO RESPONSIBILITY
AND LIMITS

♄ Q ♅

Saturn quintile Uranus:
Your Career Message:
Back to the future.

Your Hidden Talent:
Your hidden talent is your ability to build upon past structures to open the way to revolutionary thinking. You are disciplined in your approach to innovation, willing to work patiently towards those future goals. You know that innovation is based upon the work of those before you. Therefore, you don't shun the traditions of the past; you appreciate the hard work of those who have preceded you, and you use their work to support your future goals.

You value education because it opens the doors to a freedom of thought based on facts; therefore, you make sure you get the training you need. You are intelligent and forward-thinking and prefer to work with serious and dependable individuals who think the way you do. Your involvement with like-minded colleagues supports and encourages your innovative ideas.

Your strength is that your original and groundbreaking ideas are expressed in practical terms. Above all, it has to be useful. Others see you as a dependable, thoughtful, and serious innovator, not the wild-haired, crazy-eyed inventor promoting a "flux capacitor," so they take you seriously.

Because you are innovatively disciplined, you may find that future explorations into the fields of science, mathematics, and technology call to you. You may be drawn to the mechanics of aviation or to the control seat in flying vehicles.

Whatever you choose to do, discipline is an essential part of your life, and because you value time, you don't waste it. You are here to work steadily and purposefully towards the goals that you set. You understand that true freedom comes from discipline and structure, from that focus and clarity that opens the way for sudden inspirations. You need to fulfill that inner obligation to teach others and lead them on a future path. In you, it is "back to the future."

You are the conservative serious rebel. Sounds like an oxymoron, but it works for you. For within those narrow valleys of thought through which you fly, you experience unexpected storms of intuition, flashes of light that illuminate your way into the future. You are the rock and the lighthouse combined, guiding others to their starry ports of call.

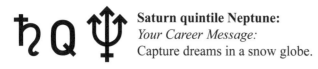

Saturn quintile Neptune:
Your Career Message:
Capture dreams in a snow globe.

Your Hidden Talent:
You have the ability to focus your attention on and give form to your vast imagination. Extremely creative, you are here to search for practical applications for the insights you have into the unseen world of mysticism and dreams. You should use your hidden talent in visible ways.

You could be a writer of fantasy novels whose heroine takes responsibility for the weaker segments of the population or the alchemist who secretly consorts with the little people of the land to bring down the evil dictator. If you choose the arts, your creative talents will carry this theme of responsibility and commitment for those in need.

You are the sensitive teacher, the example, who can communicate how necessary it is to take responsibility and give voice to the segment of society in need. You are willing to work behind the scenes, alone if necessary, to achieve your goals of social compassion. You're not afraid of hard work and you need to follow your well-laid plans to their conclusion.

You have an uncanny sense, a psychic awareness that allows you to solve mysteries and discover information that has been hidden. You would make a formidable chess player, anticipating your opponent's move almost before that opponent has given it thought. Strategy is your strong suit. You know how to maneuver behind the scenes, how to build a solid foundation, a plan of action, which can eventually achieve your goal of helping others.

You have the ability to quiet and focus your mind. Time set aside for meditation should be on your schedule. During these periods, you will have access to your imagination where you can lift the veil that separates this world from the next, a place where you can capture your visions in a snow globe.

Unlike many, you are meant to retain these fleeting images and bring them into your physical world where they become the motivation for your life. You are here to speak through your work, to enlighten the world to their spiritual responsibilities. You are the builder of storybook castles. You are the magician who sweeps the dust from the eyes of the unbelievers.

You are Gandalf whose jewel at the top of his wooden staff lights up at his command. Show the world your magic.

 **Saturn quintile Pluto:**
Your Career Message:
The tortoise wins the race.

Your Hidden Talent:
You're here to prove to the world that indeed the tortoise wins the race. Your hidden talent is that you have the patience to plan carefully to achieve the results you want. You are in for the long haul, and you are willing to work hard for a position of power. You can succeed by disciplining your mind and gathering the necessary information to reach that mountaintop.

You can be successful. It's not like a lightning strike etches your destiny in flaming letters on the road before you. Your destiny is presented more like wedged messages carved into stone posts that promise success if you walk that road step-by-step, observing the landscape along the way. By following the rules and exercising your legendary patience, you reach the goals you have set for yourself.

Your plan is based on education. Your knowledge will open fields such as finance, science, mathematics, engineering, healing, ecology, and metaphysics—professions in which you can bring about fundamental change that will affect society.

You need a position of power where you can the make major changes necessary to support and sustain the group dynamic. One support system is money. As the song goes, "Money makes the world go around . . . A mark, a yen, a buck, or a pound . . ." (*Cabaret* soundtrack). However, if you live on an island, your "money" could be cows and pigs. It's not the medium of exchange that matters, but the responsibility you feel for the protection of "money" as a support system.

You understand that the management of resources is necessary to sustain life. This goal could lead you to a profession where you work to protect the bounty of this planet's water, air, wildlife, and food sources. You realize they are not limitless, so they must be addressed.

In the magical cauldron of your mind, you are able, as one novelist wrote, to mix "facts, clues, logic, instincts, and experience" to arrive at profound insights. You feel it's your obligation, once you reach the pinnacle of success, to use your power position to bring about responsible fundamental changes in areas that support a sustainable life for the future.

You are here to show the world that dogged determination wins the race.

♄ Q ASC

Your Hidden Talent:
You do windows. You have a talent for polishing your window so cleanly every morning that not one tiny speck will impair your view. Your daily approach to life is crystal clear.

When you speak, you do so deliberately so that your point will be understood. You are able to define your messages through selectively chosen words. Too many words and too much conversation muddy the waters. You have probably given out copies of *How to Get Your Point Across in Sixty Seconds* to your more wordy friends and have introduced them to haiku as well. Certainly you suggested that concise guide, *Robert's Rules of Order*, to those you encounter on a daily basis. Laws were made for a reason.

Your range of information may be narrower than most, but what you know you have thoroughly researched so you have a deeper understanding of the subjects in your field of interest. Because you can back up your conversation, you have the respect of others. They know they can rely on your accuracy and professionalism.

Your mind doesn't dance with fairies and sugar plums; rather it dances a ballet of disciplined movements and critical thinking. Although . . . if you did decide to loosen the bonds a bit and attend a Halloween party, you would go robed as Father Time.

Time is important to you; you do not waste it because you have schedules to keep and obligations to fill. You don't go rushing about in life like the White Rabbit crying: "Oh dear! Oh dear! I shall be too late!"

Through your organizational abilities, you are here to use your creative ideas to build secure structures. You see walls and limits and laws and things that are old and proven as the bedrock of society. Your window on the world looks out upon a shiny well-ordered grid where schedules are to be met, work is to be done, and things are to be built.

You can be recognized as the person who has a sound moral compass, one who can be counted on to do the right thing because you stand upon your principles and one whose ideas can contribute to the bedrock of society . . . in spite of your lost Halloween weekend.

URANUS SPEAKS TO INDIVIDUALITY AND FREEDOM

Uranus quintile Neptune:
Peer Group Message:
Wear the same hat.

Your Peer Groups' Talents:
Your generation is here to stand for the rights of the individual to speak freely while expressing compassion for the benefit of humanity.

Your generations' talent is the ability to tap into instincts and dreams where creative insights reside. You stand for truth against any organization that would dictate the way you should live and think. You band together with those who feel the same and express your beliefs through the spoken and written word.

You are drawn to metaphysical and spiritual groups who understand that each individual has the right to live freely and in harmony with all other creatures. You may even join the Freedom from Religion Foundation because structured religions preach specific beliefs that separate its members from others who do not embrace those values. Wars are fought over which color hat the god is wearing.

An old African story tells of a god, wearing a two-colored hat, who is walking down the road in an open field. The tribe on the left side of the road exclaims, "There goes our god wearing a red hat." At the same time, the tribe of the right side of the road protests, "No! That is our god and he's wearing a green hat!" The two tribes go to war over the color of the god's hat. Many wars are fought over cultural interpretations of "who" the Creator is and how "he" functions.

You see the red-and-green hat as one hat. Your purpose is to awaken people to the truth of universal compassion and acceptance of others so that people aren't led blindly off the cliff like herds of frightened cattle during a thunderstorm. You are meant to free them from the damnation teachings of narrow established views that preach adherence to strict rules or burn in Hell forever.

Professionally, you are here to use your unique creative insights to teach compassion and joy . . . to teach that we should treat others as we would have those others treat us. You are here to speak up for the truth that we are all truly One.

 **Uranus quintile Pluto:**
Peer Group Message:
Free expression transforms the world.

Your Peer Groups' Talents:
Your peer group is here to express its right to speak freely in pursuit of progressive change, to speak out against the powerful forces that seek to control the individual through financial, legal, and governmental power.

You rebel against large sums of money and power placed in the hands of the few through which they determine the destiny of the populace. These plutocrats who seek to dominate the world through eliminating the independence of the people will have a fight on their hands. Your generation has the courage and deep commitment to add voices to the fight against those who would oppress the individual.

Your talent lies in your ability to put into words what your generation desires. You are heard at every political public forum, you voice your opinion to your representatives, you gather forces to reject government legislation that benefits only the rich and powerful, and you do all this in the service of uprooting hidden agendas that strive to put power in the hands of the few to the detriment of the many.

You demand freedom in your pursuit of basic resources needed to support the needs of society to function regardless of basic differences. Political freedom, sexual freedom, and the freedom of privacy are your deep motivations.

Those who would work in secret to undermine those liberties will have to contend with your generation's voice crying for liberty. If that voice is not heard, there will be revolution, governments will topple, leaders will be exposed, the mighty will fall.

Through digging deep into the underpinnings of life, the psychological motivations of humans, the secrets of nature, your generation will, through innovative and independent thinking, emerge with inventive discoveries that will affect humanity for the better.

You are here to tear down outworn, negative, destructive institutions through revolution if necessary, and to replace them with fresh new perspectives embodied in new institutions and laws that point to a future of individual responsibility for the whole. You will not be muffled; you will be heard, and those in power should heed that voice or it will lead to their demise.

♅ Q ASC

Your Hidden Talent:

Your window to the world is wide open, no screens allowed. Who knows what's going to fly in, and besides, you're already dressed to fly out.

Probably, by the age of five, you were studying the ephemeris, that magical book that lists the planets' locations for every day, or you were mixing "under-the-sink chemicals" to provide the power to boost the rocket you made out of tinfoil, or you were composing symphonies in crayon on pads of scrap paper.

To say that you look at the world through a different window is putting it mildly. You are here to use that rebellious mind that continually questions what is and what can be. You should not bow to current thought if it doesn't make sense to you. You may have found it difficult through your early education to follow traditional methods of learning because your intuitive mind makes leaps of logic beyond what others are thinking at that moment.

You think outside the box, outside the limits that others deem possible. Your conversations are never ordinary; your mind is stimulated every day when you open the window on your environment. You see new possibilities. Literally, the sky's the limit! You may even own a telescope because who know what you can discover gazing into that starry abode.

Others may see you as eccentric and unique but always fascinating. You add excitement and sparkle to any conversation. This makes you a welcome addition to any gathering. Let the games begin!

Even though you have an unusual way of communicating, you are intuitive enough to understand how you are coming across to others and what piques their interest. This ability will serve you well in any profession you choose. You have the talent to stimulate the mind of the public through your inventive ideas.

You are here to work from a visible platform where the extremely creative ideas and images that pop into your restless mind are translated into a message for the world. You see things clearly, and from a position of leadership, you can stimulate creative thinking in others. You can be recognized as an innovative and exciting leader, one who represents the possibilities of what the future holds.

NEPTUNE SPEAKS TO COMPASSION, IMAGINATION, AND WISDOM

Neptune quintile Pluto:
Generational Message:
Compassionate transformation.

Your Generation's Talents:
Your generation is here to express compassion for the welfare of those in need by bringing about fundamental change to the crumbling laws and institutions that were meant to help them.

You recognize that it is time to tear down old structures that have outlived their usefulness and have turned against the downtrodden. The greed and need for power and the domination of governments and financial institutions to control the world have met their match. You will speak through your better angels to send the message of compassionate inclusiveness.

Your generation has an obsessive need to give voice to the poor who have no voice and no control over their lives, an intense need to lift the light beside their doors to shine on their dreams of welcome in the spiritual community of life.

The universal expression of compassion and the push for spiritual meaning beyond the dictates of organized belief systems and structures will wash away negative power. Compassion and spirituality are universal truths, the essential meaning of life, the final destination of lives lived, the meeting of endings and new beginnings. It is the cycle of life and will not be denied.

You need to show the world that when you pick a flower, you disturb a star, to let them know that each life is a precious gift that has the potential to create beauty in this world. Your words are weapons that free the mystical side of life from the dungeons of control so that people can express their belief in the invisible but real world of the imagination where angels hold court, a place where they can achieve the promise of their dreams in fantasy or in reality.

Your generation can release this creative expression through spiritual expressions in which we become cognizant of the invisible world beyond the physical plane, where things that cannot be seen still exist and are believed in.

You are involved in new movements that stretch beyond the five senses, where metaphysical teachings hold the reins of power—subjects like psychic ability, ESP, and clairvoyance that reveal other planes of "reality." Here your generation teaches that physics meets metaphysics.

 **Neptune quintile Ascendant:**
Your Career Message:
Turn on your fog lights.

Your Hidden Talent:

You don't have to turn on your fog lights when you get up in the morning. They're on high beams already. You love the misty look at life, for it is within this watery view your imagination plays with the dew drops.

Your talent is your sensitivity to your environment. This started early in your life when you may have had imaginary playmates. They were ready to play when you opened your eyes every morning. The adults around you said they were imaginary, but you knew they were real. You were in touch with a world beyond the physical.

As you grew, you empathized so strongly with those people in your environment that you began to feel what they were feeling. You sense things: your English teacher had a bad day because of a fight with her husband that morning; the clerk in the grocery store with the secret smile on her face just found out she was pregnant; your closest friend is planning a surprise birthday party for you.

You tend to daydream, off into your own world of fantasy. You pick up on the slightest nuances in your environment and then you're off, imagining what that might mean and spinning creative images around it. You marvel at the dandelion fluff picked up by a passing breeze and the iridescent colors of the butterfly as it dances by.

You feel a flutter in your heart when you asked the little neighbor boy if he was going to hunt Easter eggs, to which he replied with the light of joyful innocence shining in his eyes, "The Easter Bunny came last night and left me a package."

Your imagination has no boundaries. You are here to give a voice to your visions, to find a public platform from which your creativity can be expressed and applauded. You may find the mystical arts your home, or you may immerse yourself in the field of charitable work, dreams, and healing, or as the leader of retreats where your boundless imagination can lift others. From your public position you elevate the boundless faith and joy of a child who still believes all things are possible.

When those naysayers delare, "You can't believe in impossible things," you quote the white queen's response to Alice, "I daresay you haven't had much practice . . . why sometimes I've believed as many as six impossible things before breakfast!"

PLUTO SPEAKS TO
FUNDAMENTAL TRANSFORMATION

 **Pluto quintile Ascendant:**
Your Career Message:
See through walls.

Your Hidden Talent:
As a child you peered through a shadowy window that loved mysteries and detective stories, spy movies, and games where the protagonist digs up secret clues that eventually expose the truth. Maybe you played *Dungeons and Dragons*® as a kid—you would have loved that title—words that implied the underworld and things that go bump in the night.

Today, like the Shaolin priest, you can see though, rather than walk through, walls. You pick up on nuances—maybe it's the sweaty brow, the shift of the eyes, the nervous fingers, the false smile, the insincere words—that are what's called "the tell." Your built-in lie detector sets off alarms at the slightest falsehoods.

Your talent is your ability to look at the world through this powerful lens. Because you probe beneath the surface of everyday affairs, very little gets past you. Your thought processes run deep, getting to the bottom of any situation you are examining. Investigating and uncovering hidden information is right up your alley.

Because your words carry weight, a result of your deep investigation into any given subject, you gain the respect of others and thereby influence public thinking on important issues that have far-reaching effects. You understand that words have the power to bring down moldering institutions. You are here to put every last ounce of your energy into achieving these goals.

Once you have entered into an agreement, your word is your bond. You understand that once you sign your name to a document of any kind, you are bound to those rules. You know the far-reaching impact that documents have upon the social, economic, religious, and political landscape; you will fight any injustices you find there.

The signers of the Declaration of Independence vowed to fight for life, liberty, and the pursuit of happiness in the face of losing all they owned. You know the global consequences of that simple document. Your purpose is to stand behind what you say. Your words matter; they can change the world.

THE SESQUIQUINTILE ASPECTS

THE TEN PLANETS
AND THE ASCENDANT

THE MOON SPEAKS TO YOUR EMOTIONS AND NURTURING INSTINCTS

$$\text{☽} \; D^3 \; \text{☉}$$

Moon sesquiquintile Sun:
Your Legacy:
The light of your imagination.

Discover Your DNA Treasure:
You are a person whose identity is automatically attached to a creative accomplishment. You prove that the individual's creative imagination can live on as an inspiration for others, opening the creative flow of talent into the world. When we speak the name Mozart, we think sonatas; Leonardo da Vinci, we think the *Mona Lisa*; Mary Shelley we think Frankenstein; Robert Louis Stevenson, we think Dr. Jekyll.

It's time to manifest your creative identity. Who you are, your face and your name, will be recognized. You represent a prehistory replete with talented individuals who may not have been recognized or recorded in the libraries of time. You are here to make the headlines—to reach around the world through your deep desire to nurture individual creativity. You stand as the beacon for enlightened movements, progressive publications, groundbreaking legal decisions, and artistic renewals.

People see you as self-confident, a person who is comfortable with who you are and how to get what you desire. There is no resentment here. The harmonious flow between your inner emotional world and your outer identity shines through you. You are comfortable in your own skin, as they say. Others are magnetically drawn to you. The ease with which you accept others creates an environment where people feel secure and happy in your presence. People just plain like you.

You do need time in your chosen sanctuary where you are able to nurture your creative roots; you then emerge into the world with a healthy ego, ready to shine in the world.

Your gift to the world is an optimistic and broad view of the individual's creative potential. This attitude opens minds so others can also reach for the stars. You are the shining example of what they can become. The light of your vitality and optimism restores faith in those who have lost it, gives hope to those who have none, and gives joy to those who hear you. You stand as an example of what their possibilities are if they have faith in themselves. You have come to uncover your DNA treasure and shine the light into your hidden library where all your experiences are stored so they can be shared with future generations.

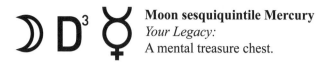

Moon sesquiquintile Mercury
Your Legacy:
A mental treasure chest.

Discover Your DNA Treasure:
You are the embodiment of Rodin's nude bronze sculpture, *The Thinker*, deep in thought, stripped of the layers of civilization that hide the inner truths. You are here to send a message to the world that the mind is a treasure that must be protected and allowed to grow.

Your caring intellect is the treasure you will present to the world. You not only give voice to and acknowledge the contributions of the past, but your prophetic view of the future is based upon your prenatal knowledge, a good case for past-life remembrances. You connect back through time, listening to the voices of your past perhaps through dreams or meditation where you pick up the threads of your linear history. From there creative ideas spring forth.

You understand humanity's need for philosophies and belief systems that offer cohesion and connection, but at the same time, you make the case for expanding the more rigid views of society. You see the trend of the current thought patterns in the world and introduce new concepts that have been lingering on the edges, waiting to wake up the world mind.

You verbalize your nurturing instincts through teaching moral lessons through your chosen methods. You speak a broader message that allows the mind to grow beyond tribal thinking.

Your name is associated with a deep desire to protect and educate through communication. Examples like Montessori education, named after the Italian physician and educator Maria Montessori, which highlights the students choice of activity and allows uninterrupted periods of work time. Language and education are food for your soul.

Spending time in quiet places, talking to your subconscious, tugging on that thread that links you to your past, listening to the voices from before, these are the techniques that enrich your life and uncover the treasure that has been passed down to you through your mitochondrial DNA, from your mother. You tap into your Akashic records, the cosmic library of your mind where your talent carries your message to the world—nurture and enlighten others.

What are you waiting for? The pen is mightier than the sword.

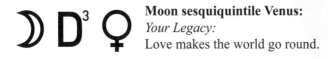

Moon sesquiquintile Venus:
Your Legacy:
Love makes the world go round.

Discover Your DNA Treasure:
You are here to manifest love and its healing art.

There's an old saying that you catch more flies with honey than vinegar. Actually, honey is healing. Imhotep, revered physician to ancient pharaohs, used honey as an antibiotic to heal, instinctively recognizing it as a substance in which bacteria can't grow. Honey is called the "sweetest antibiotic." It's also effective on burns.

You instinctively know that a "honeyed" approach heals relationships. Through the art of compromise, you smooth the flames of anger. Effective in public relations, your empathy and gentleness radiate out to "soothe the savage beast."

Your voice has a soothing quality that serves you well in sending your message of love and harmony to humanity, the message that "love makes the world go round." At heart, you always have the best intentions towards the other person. You brighten the world around you. Most likely you dislike coarse language and bad manners because of your natural desire for beauty and harmony in your world.

You have a strong artistic bent and could find the theater as a place of self-expression where you can exercise the sweet harmony of your voice. Your words can find voice in poetry, or your sense of beauty and balance may express in the field of interior design, the beauty of landscaping, the love of domesticity.

You're the Queen Bee residing over your treasure hive where love resides in the honeycombed chambers of your soul. The bees build their hives using the most efficient use of space: the six-sided hexagon. Interestingly, six is the number of love, balance, and harmony. You understand nature's message: If people are to share the space they occupy in this life in the most efficient manner, they should work together to build a better world hive through love and cooperation.

So, you continue your work of spreading a little honey on the bread of life, and you give thanks to your coworkers, the busy bees, for working in harmony and cooperation to pollinate the earth. You both present the "sweetest antibiotic" to humanity, the gift of love.

 **Moon sesquiquintile Mars:**
Your Legacy:
Indestructible metal bracelets.

Discover Your DNA Treasure:
Somewhere in your history was a line of warrior women. Rather than inheriting great-grandma's diamond ring and complete twelve-piece setting of sterling silver, you received a set of indestructible metal bracelets. You are meant to wear these "Bracelets of Submission" that give you the power to submit to and absorb the incoming attacks from the world and, through emotional control, balance and strengthen the human ego.

Like Wonder Woman, you're the warrior, fighting for family, home, and world community. It's built into your DNA to be dedicated and passionate, to take action to right a wrong, to protect the threatened and the resources they require to live in safety. One way to do this is through the legal system in the halls of justice.

Legislation that seeks to ensure that professions like police, fire, the military, and the health industry are able to carry on in the true spirit of "serve and protect" have your full and active support. You may have opponents but they never question your belief that your agenda is for the protection of all. You can also energize others to join your cause.

Because you understand human behavior and feel impelled to take action when things appear to be going awry, you step in and instinctively apply the correct amount of pressure required by situations that arise.

You do have an enterprising instinct that serves you well in building up businesses that have to do with the home and the world community and its health and well-being—all those services that protect the larger population.

Through the efficient use of your energy, you always have a reserve, a pool to draw from. However, you do need periods of retreat when you can reinvigorate not only your creativity but your body as well. Practices such as Tai Chi and yoga stimulate your creative juices. The emotional impacts of great works of art feed your soul and encourage you to make your own contributions to beauty in this world.

Your deep commitment to the ideal of home and country will be remembered in the annals of history. You will be remembered as that woman who wore those shiny bracelets and fought the good fight.

☽ D³ ♃   **Moon sesquiquintile Jupiter:**
Your Legacy:
Boundless imagination.

Discover Your DNA Treasure:
Your boundless imagination is the DNA treasure you awaken in this life. You are here to inspire the masses with your creative expertise. You may expound from the pulpit, the court, or the ivy-covered halls of academia; but rest assured, you will be recognized and valued for your message.

Through your creative imagination you lift the public consciousness into higher realms of awareness. Your positive outlook on life spreads hope and happiness. You may take others on a journey "around the world in 80 days" through your writings, travelogues, public relations, and civic connections, where your optimistic views expand what the public believes is possible.

You are successful and may be wealthy. Some people think success is luck, but it is often the result of confidence and positive thinking. What we send out comes back: the law of physics. You see opportunities everywhere; your imagination expands those possibilities. You may require a well-appointed sanctuary, a comfortable environment where you can fuel your imagination.

Einstein said: "The true sign of intelligence is not knowledge but imagination." Bingo! You have both!

Scott Adams, creator of the *Dilbert* cartoon strip, posed the question: "If imagination is the foundation of emotional intelligence and emotional intelligence is the biggest factor in success, shouldn't we be training kids to better imagine their futures?" Since you understand the answer to this question, you have always worked towards that goal.

Your generous nature and warm personality welcome others into your fold. You are the Big Mama, the mentor who's willing to help others through your glass overflowing philosophy. You show others how to fill their glasses and then inspire them to let their overflow pay-it-forward to help others.

You show by example that living an honorable life, true to your highest principles, can bring wealth and fame. But you're also a believer in to whom much is given, much is expected. You give generously of your talent, your imagination, your knowledge, and your experience. These are the attributes for which you will be long remembered.

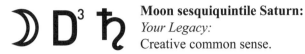

Moon sesquiquintile Saturn:
Your Legacy:
Creative common sense.

Discover Your DNA Treasure:

Your past experiences taught you to justify taking up space in the world, and now you have that talent to offer to the world at large. You are here to teach others to use their cautious conservative natures creatively, to bask in the dignity of responsibility, to imagine the future based upon the past.

You are here to build stone castles, not lined with drafty cold halls, but with rooms filled with freshly baked warm bread. You use your engineering skills to build comfortable structures that provide emotional support. Rather than discard the past, you value the work of your predecessors and you build upon existing laws and imagine more possibilities. You visualize a secure and useful future built upon the well-tested traditions of the past.

You need periods of silence and a place of retreat where you can be alone to imagine and build.

You may be involved in repairing or supporting venerable old institutions like libraries or government facilities where the knowledge of the past is preserved for future eyes. You may write stories about those who struggle with their past and then rise with dignity. You place one well-crafted stone upon another, building secure walls internally within the mind or externally for the world body.

Your brilliance is your common sense. You take that which is already established and proven, strip it to its essence, and then, using your creative imagination, build upon and expand that elemental structure. You literally see in your mind's eye what it can become.

The definition of mind's eye is "the place where visual images are conjured up from memory . . ." This talent of yours comes from your DNA/past-life experiences, the linear thread that connects you to what you already know and are.

Discipline is your comfort level. Your emotions are in check, you remain cool and focused on the road ahead. You work patiently and ignore the doubts of the naysayers. Your prescience, your foreknowledge of what can be built before others recognize the possibilities, is that for which you will be remembered.

$$\text{☽ } D^3 \text{ ⛢}$$

Moon sesquiquintile Uranus:
Your Legacy:
The unfettered imagination.

Discover Your DNA Treasure:

Your family history is unusual. Some of your ancestors most likely had the "second sight," were closet clairvoyants, or astrologers. Your treasure comes from a prehistory of futuristic imaginings. You are here to manifest your second sight.

Second sight is defined as the power to see beyond the range of ordinary perception. Think about the words separately . . . second and sight. This means you don't accept circumstances the way they appear on the surface; you instinctively take a second look.

This is your strength, your creative talent. You break barriers with your flashes of insight and intuition that stem from an original imagination that is tuned to the future. You need sequestered time to nurture your boundless and perhaps technically tuned imagination to make breakthroughs. Your dreams may be prophetic. So many advances in human history have come through dreams.

You seek truth from beneath the surface, in the hidden world of nature, of human behavior, of issues that affect the public needs. You are a champion for those truths that illuminate the dark corners of the mind.

Your imagination produces "faster than a speeding bullet"; you're a superwoman of the imagination. Advertising agencies would love to have you on their payroll, not only for these perceptions, but also for your ability to tap into future trends to see what the public will want and need.

You add sparkle to any gathering; people never know what they're going to get. You are comfortable with strange ideas that others never entertain. Your "wondering" knows no limits: What would it be like to "ride alongside a light beam"? What secrets can flowers impart? What changes would occur if you rearranged accepted formulae?

You nurture the imagination of people around the world through your innovative work, which opens their minds to possibilities. You excite and perhaps unsettle people. Sometimes they feel you can read their minds.

You seek truth in the hidden world of nature, and human behavior. Your contribution to the world stands as testament to these principles.

Moon Sesquiquintile Neptune:
Your Legacy:
The music of the spheres.

Discover Your DNA Treasure:

Through your DNA, you are tuned in to the music of the spheres and you come to manifest your talent.

Spiritually uplifting music transports you to ethereal realms. You are exceptionally talented when it comes to the arts, and music in particular expresses the compassion and deep feelings that flow from your inner treasure trove. You are here to uplift the souls of others.

You are the poet, the romantic who envisions "knights in white satin," the belief that fairy tales can come true. The breadth of your imagination is astounding.

You sense the shifting moods of the public, their spiritual needs as apart from their religious beliefs, and your dream of bringing people together under one creative umbrella is the gift you give to the world. Through the universal language of the arts, especially music and the joy of graceful movement, you touch generations.

You are so sensitive to your surroundings that you absorb the slightest nuances and emotional shifts in others so that your psychic antenna is always in flux. Their inner thoughts, feelings, and emotions involuntarily flow over you. You feel their connections between the physical and spiritual worlds, which can result in mediumistic tendencies.

You are genuinely accepting of people. Your gentle nature wraps others in a warm blanket of safety. You care deeply about the needs of others, which you may express as a therapist or counselor. Because of your deep compassion for humanity, you might work within other spiritually inclined groups to assist those in need.

Retreats are important. You need away time in secluded sanctuaries where you can detach from the distractions of the busy world, secret places where you absorb the beauty that nature has to offer, where you reconnect with fairies and angels and fantasies, where "pollen floating in water proves the existence of atoms."

Your gift, your legacy, is your powerful imagination, your emotional sensitivity, and your compassion, which you give generously to the world.

Moon sesquiquintile Pluto:
Your Legacy:
Raise the drawbridge.

Discover Your DNA Treasure:

"It's not nice to fool Mother Nature!" That line from an old Chiffon Margarine commercial depicts an angry Mother Nature deep in the woods, surrounded by her critters, bringing down her wrath with bolts of lightning after being fooled into thinking she was eating butter.

You are here to manifest your strength and your emotional intensity in public view. You won't be fooled—you can't be fooled—because you have insight beyond most. You know how things work in the physical world because you understand how things work sub-atomically. You know cause and effect, and where there is a cause you will work tirelessly to bring about the effect.

It's almost magical the way you approach and solve problems. You have a secret laboratory buried in the bowels of the castle where foaming glass tubes and wing of bat and eye of newt clutter the wooden benches. You're the Cosmic Mother performing earth alchemy. You need periods of retreat to this sanctuary.

You're like many mothers, psychically tuned in, with those eyes in the back of your head that cause children so much angst. Your feelings run deep, and you pit your formidable will to bringing about fundamental change to structures that are decaying from within, especially when those institutions threaten the security and well-being of the human family and the Earth.

Tearing down negative power structures provides fodder for you to use for reconstruction and rehabilitation. You may do this on the physical level through the healing arts, such as physical and/or psychological therapy, or legally through sweeping legislation that protects and ensures the safety of family and foods, or financially through protecting the savings and retirement plans of the public. You're particularly adept at handling and managing large sums of money.

You know you are here to change life for the better of humanity. You are familiar with power and you're comfortable with it. You understand human motivations. You don't need mantras in the morning or clever quotes hanging on your walls. These philosophies are deeply embedded in your DNA.

You are here to do a job, and you will do it come hell or high water! And people will know who you are.

☽ D³ ASC

Moon sesquiquintile Ascendant:
Your Legacy:
Myths and fairy tales.

Discover Your DNA Treasure:

You are the mythical storyteller. Your roots run deep into your past-life experiences where you have witnessed the power of myths and beliefs. Your vast imagination is a storehouse from which you evoke images that resonate within others.

You recognize that these simple fairy tales, childhood rhymes, and Olympian myths that have persisted down through the ages are still part and parcel of today's body of knowledge. However, you realize that most people miss the point of these stories.

You understand that these stories, more than just words, reach into the depths of the unconscious, and pull up images that leave lasting impressions. You weave your tales with ease, inviting your audience to listen to memories past. You remind people of the value of their beliefs and help them see that all beliefs are interwoven by a common thread.

People identify with your stories because they intuit the universal moral hidden within the parables. They begin to see the truths that you impart and that opens their minds and eyes to a new look at their own lives. You change their perceptions and broaden their windows on the world. They then awaken to each day with a clearer vision of what life offers.

You understand the emotional needs of cultures to connect to something greater than themselves and their personal lives, the need to feel part of a larger cosmic plan. You know that intelligence is based upon the depth of knowledge rather than the surface rituals that often detract from the truth. You guide them gently through simple stories that hide powerful lessons.

You may travel the world by vehicles absorbing cultures, or you may travel by winged armchair. However, you always return to your quiet sanctuary to connect with what you already know.

You are here to manifest your creative expression through teaching the simple moral lessons that are hidden in plain sight. You may do this as a parent, teacher, speaker, writer, social advocate—any platform that gives you an audience. Your legacy gives comfort to the public mind through your vast library of myths, fairy tales, and legends.

THE SUN SPEAKS TO YOUR IDENTITY

⊙ D³ ♂   **Sun sesquiquintile Mars:**
Your Legacy:
Courage.

Discover Your DNA Treasure:
You come from a line of warrior kings. It's time to manifest your talent as a natural leader. Unafraid to tackle difficult problems or to fight the good fight, you embrace adversity with confidence and faith in yourself. You have the soul of a warrior, and it's time to feel the flush of success and recognition.

You are identified with courage, because you won't give up. You pursue your goals with a seemingly unending supply of energy. You instinctively know how to moderate your activities, a practice that keeps you going long after others are dropping by the wayside. You know "how to hold them" but you "never fold them" because your keen sense of timing aids you in selecting the battles that you are prepared for. You've been tested. Now you have a secure base upon which to launch yourself in pursuit of your objective.

Self-directed, you focus on what you want to achieve. You enjoy challenges and pursue them with enthusiasm. What you do and how you lead reflects on your identity. You are aware of your role as an example for others, so honesty and fair play are hallmarks of your life.

You use your creative ability assertively and with purpose but you don't challenge people . . . rather you sweep them up in your cause. Your invigorating spirit and vitality infects them as well. They feel motivated under your leadership.

You know how to direct your desires, and you don't approve of those who lose their tempers or are unable to contain their aggressive instincts. You see that as a fruitless waste of energy. You stand as the one who uses your drive to achieve with dignity.

You will step in when someone needs a hand because you are secure in your identity. Your self-confidence leaves room for others to enjoy success as well.

Not prone to violence, you still have an inborn courage and confidence to handle conflict and to live the life you have chosen. You are a pioneer, forging new paths of exploration and placing your personal stamp on the journey. That stamp is marked with originality, decisiveness, courage, and endurance.

☉ D³ ♃ **Sun sesquiquintile Jupiter:**
Your Legacy:
Fiery optimism.

Discover Your DNA Treasure:
The sky's the limit, and you are here to finally make a name for yourself and shine in that domain. You came into this life with an abundance of qualifications; now you must choose the venue through which to manifest those talents so that your presence here on Earth will inspire future generations.

The fire in your personality and the breadth of your knowledge will find a platform from which to shine. Your optimistic philosophy will light up whatever profession you choose. From the pulpit of religion, politics, the legal profession, teaching, writing, counseling, the theater, or the healing arts, you hold the "bully pulpit," the opportunity to speak out on any issues you hold dear.

Just like the white queen in "Through the Looking Glass," you believe in achieving "impossible things before breakfast" if you put your heart into the dream. You inspire that same philosophy in the breasts of others through your magnetism and youthful exuberance which embodies the belief that all things are possible. The child in you still believes in impossible things.

You do need time to contemplate, to retreat to that quiet sanctum where you can indulge yourself in the pursuit of knowledge, surrounded by your DNA cosmic library, your links to your prehistory. In this sanctuary you connect to your lineage and are replenished and supported in your efforts to shine a light on broadening people's education.

Your generosity in helping others goes to the heart of what you do. Regardless of your profession, you believe that knowledge is the right of all people; therefore, libraries and institutions of learning should be available to people from all walks of life. You support the free distribution of books and support free libraries around the world. It is within these hallowed halls that people can learn to touch the Sun. Your name may well be associated with such places.

Your reputation spreads beyond the confines of your local community, because you represent the yearning to breathe fresher air, to live with more purpose, to reach for one's identity at higher elevations where the view is spectacular. This is your destiny this lifetime.

Sun sesquiquintile Saturn:
Your Legacy:
Timeless structures.

Discover Your DNA Treasure:

You come from a long history of master builders. With a square and compass in hand, you are here to use your skills to continue to build institutions that will endure as a light for future generations.

You are laser focused on the work you do. You plant a seed, and through your hard work, discipline, and concentration, you see to its well-being. That seed then begins to spiral out in a consistent steady manner like the growth of the nautilus, the curve from its central point spreading outward to encompass the globe in mathematical precision.

You gather the tools you need to assist your practical efforts. No work day is too long; no job too tough. It is through your single-handed focus on a goal and through your management skills that you manage to drum up the resources you need to accomplish your ends. You never run short because you have planned ahead. People may marvel at the ease with which you overcome obstacles in order to finish the job.

You take to heart Aseop's statement: "Implementation beats oration." And you certainly believe that if you want a job done right, do it yourself. That's why you do the job yourself. You trust your own skills to follow through to the end. Therefore, you oversee the work of those involved in your building projects.

The precision with which you construct your world speaks of the love you have for what you build. Organization and conservation are key words in your lexicon. You see beauty in simplicity, in clean lines that speak more than ostentatious displays.

You "work locally but think globally." You want to leave something of value behind for others. Your work contains a lasting message for the world with those who have eyes to see.

It has been said that the Great Pyramid is a book in stone. Through its geometrical construction and mathematical precision it has left a message written in form and number.

It's time for you to grab your tools and live up to Gibran's beautiful line: "Work is love made visible." Your identity lives on, perhaps engraved in marble faces.

Sun sesquiquintile Uranus:
Your Legacy:
Shine for freedom.

Discover Your DNA Treasure:

You are here to manifest the principle of freedom, to complete some task that links your name with the desire of all humanity to break free from the chains that bind. Your prehistory has suited you well for this destiny. Any wild haired starry-eyed misfits in your ancestry?

You will not follow the trodden path of blind history or mindlessly repeat the accepted teachings of the past if your view is obstructed. Like the eagle whose eyesight is three times sharper than that of humans and can spot dinner from several miles away or a hawk who can see his meal from a height of 15,000 feet and then dive at 100 mph completely focused on that target, you have a clear vision of your goal.

You think way outside the box. Most people regard you as a bit askew, different, unusual, even rebellious because you challenge the status quo. You question why things should stay the way they are. You are the one person who will stand up against the barriers that restrict moving into the future. You want to make room for public discourse from all cultures and their beliefs. You understand that the world needs to be rocked upon occasion, and you're the one who can do it. Your hand rocks humanity's cradle so that the world can grow up with an open mind. Should we say, "You rock!"

You do stand out; you can't help it. It's in your genes. Just because something has always been done a certain way doesn't mean you can't try a different way of doing it. You want to open doors to greater possibilities. You want the freedom to soar above conventional thought. So you question the status quo and eventually become the symbol of change.

Scientists have proven aerodynamically that the bumble bee cannot fly. But the bee doesn't know that so it goes buzzing merrily from flower to flower.

So it doesn't matter whether you're a bumble bee pollinating the food that feeds the world or a hawk soaring from great heights for food, you are here to feed freedom to the souls on this planet.

You look up and you see. This is your signature.

Leonardo da Vinci spoke of you: "Once you have tasted flight, you will forever walk the earth with your eyes turned skyward . . ."

 **Sun sesquiquintile Neptune:**
Your Legacy:
A poetic heart.

Discover Your DNA Treasure:
You have the heart of a poet and mystic. You are here to bring grace and beauty into the world, to lift the souls of those who yearn to reach "out of bounds for the ends of Being and ideal Grace." Empathy for humanity with all its foibles is your hallmark.

You are from a prehistory of visionaries fueled by imagination whose light shone on dreams of what could be in a perfect world. You carry on this tradition, only now you're to be recognized.

You do need moments of withdrawal to a private sanctuary where you replenish yourself, a time that allows your imagination to embrace the whole picture. As Einstein said, ". . . imagination embraces the entire world, and all there ever will be to know and understand." Your imagination finds nourishment in spiritual retreat where silence allows you to feel and to see through the thin veil between this world and the next.

You are extremely psychic and tuned into your feelings and the things you sense. You seem to know where to be and what to do at any given time. You're always on call. When the "aha thread" that connects you to the cosmic telephone jingles, you answer.

The gentle Hawaiian culture who historically believed in one god and treated women as equals believed the thread of awareness, the aha thread, formed a worldwide web that connected everyone. You have that telephone number.

Your imagination, empathy, and enormous creativity may manifest in music, art, theater, writing, education, and the healing arts where a spiritual component underlies your work.

As a leader in any profession, you stand out; your inner light shines brightly. You are the beacon that clears the foggy vision of those who wish to see.

Whether you represent ideals as does the Tarot's Key 9, The Hermit, on the mountaintop holding the lantern of wisdom for those to follow, or your ideals shine from a place of seclusion as Key 2, The Priestess, you will be remembered for the light of compassion and creativity you leave behind.

 **Sun sesquiquintile Pluto:**
Your Legacy:
Witchery.

Discover Your DNA Treasure:
You come from a long line of witches and wizards, those people who knew the natural laws of the Earth and used that knowledge to bring about healing change. Out of necessity, they worked their magic from behind closed doors. They wore the cloak of invisibility. You are here to cast off that cloak and carry that tradition into the open. Your name will be synonymous with the magic you weave.

You know it's time to expose the dark underbelly of society, those beliefs and practices that are so ingrained in society that they are not questioned but become second nature. You question and test and work behind the scenes—temporarily if necessary—to expose Earth's secrets. Your efforts will bring destructive issues into the light of healing.

You live your life with passion. Unafraid, you tackle monumental problems knowing that you will make a difference. You gather your forces and focus your will with an intensity that brooks no opposition. You know how to use your resources in the most efficient manner; nothing is wasted.

You have what others would call an almost "supernatural energy."

When you leave a room, people don't exclaim, "Who is that masked woman?" They know exactly who you are and the powerful change you can wreak. They see you as an irresistible force, a slow tsunami whose wave washes away the rooted "dark side" of the ingrained destructive mores of society. Nothing will be the same because you can break down barriers constructed by those who would control the lives of others.

You want the truth. You challenge the status quo if that "quo," the existing state of affairs, has created a social structure and a set of values that limits society's growth. You stand for the individual's right to control their own destiny with responsibility and right action. Your aura of vitality and self confidence draws others to your cause. They sense you are the one who will be the spearhead of change.

You are a powerful leader who has cast off your ancestor's cloak of invisibility and now stands in the Sun ready to concentrate your will power with laser-like focus on fundamental change. You are the witchy woman!

Sun sesquiquintile Ascendant:
Your Legacy:
Sunny windows.

Discover Your DNA Treasure:
You come from a long line of believers and achievers who looked through light-filled windows. You are here to promote that treasure. Your name shines as an example of what self-esteem and a positive outlook on life can achieve.

Your belief in yourself inspires confidence in others. They dream they could grow up to be you, whom they idolize as an icon of vitality and the nobility of the spirit. Your face is recognizable and immediately inspires a feeling of what is possible. In the public consciousness, your face can light up the "breakfast of champions" cereal box or your presence stands as a global message that "you can overcome."

People recognize that your childlike belief in all things possible has matured into an adult belief that all things can be possible. You have become what you thought you could be. Your philosophy rings with the belief that all things are possible. Your optimism proves the "observer effect," which postulates that in a controlled experiment the expectation of the observer slightly alters the results of the experiment. In the eyes of the world, you represent that innate expectation of winning.

In fact, when you open your eyes each morning, you look through your personal window into a world full of positive possibilities. You greet each day with vitality and the assurance that the best is about to be. Your physical presence is uplifting because you greet others with a broad smile and you carry yourself with dignity and self-esteem. Others automatically sit up and stand straighter as your bright aura envelops them.

In addition, you are generally liked for your sincerity and your friendly and generous personality. Your role as a leader rests comfortably on your shoulders because it comes so naturally. You are the presence that lifts the world into a higher more optimistic consciousness.

You are here to use your position in fields such as the performing arts, sports, education, and social media to broadcast belief in oneself through one's personal outlook on life.

Everything about you speaks success; you are the icon of a brighter future. This is your legacy to the world.

MERCURY SPEAKS TO THINKING AND COMMUNICATION

 **Mercury sesquiquintile Mars:**
Your Legacy:
Put your money where your mouth is.

Discover Your DNA Treasure:
It's built into your DNA, the competitive nature to venture on new paths, to be first to win the gold or to discover a new theory. Your family tree is heavy with the leaves of those who were feisty winners, who spoke up, who would go it alone to achieve their goals. You are here to carry on that tradition and leave your personal mark on a global field.

Your stamp on the world results from the mental energy you apply to everything you attempt. You pursue your goals with mental vigor, seeking challenging outlets. Your internal battery never runs out of juice.

Your voice, your message, your words will be heard. Communication is your weapon; victory is your goal. Your desire to explore new territory places you at the head of the pack. You don't look back to see what's behind because you are focused on what's up front.

The urge to be first and best at what you do sets you above the crowd. You will go it alone to physically or mentally achieve your goal. Your ever searching mind is your strength. Coupled with the force behind your mental processes, you will stand out in the crowd as you tirelessly pursue a line of thought or a physical regimen.

You dig into and investigate new trenches of learning, uncovering how things work in the physical world. On a practical level, you may have an interest in machines and how they operate. You may view your body as a machine that needs to be efficiently maintained and well oiled to achieve maximum operation. You could view your words as a tool to oil the gears of communication where you can exert your mental prowess.

Wherever and however you choose to apply your considerable mental energy, your purpose is to influence the public consciousness as to what is possible if just one person not only speaks but backs up her words with action.

You are here to speak up loudly and clearly, and to leave your exploits behind to energize and encourage others to follow in your pioneering footsteps. You put your money where your mouth is.

☿ D³ ♃

Mercury sesquiquintile Jupiter:
Your Legacy:
A bigger library.

Discover Your DNA Treasure:
Oh, the wondrous things you know. Well, now it's time to share.

Supported by your DNA ancestry, you are here to manifest your knowledge, to spread your creative message far and wide. You carry the mace, the wand, the staff, which symbolizes your power and jurisdiction over encoded data. You are the conductor of the accumulated thought patterns of the world. Grab your orchestral baton!

A little hyperbole, granted, but yours is a big job. Your curiosity knows no limits. You are here to build upon the accumulated wisdom of your prehistory, that of your ancestry, and your own past-life experiences, in order to add to the knowledge contained in the libraries of the world.

You are not fettered by existing rules or limits; rather, you are supported by them and seek to expand upon what is already known. You are here to express your ideas beyond what was taught to you in school, to question what others accept as truth, to turn over in your mind what you see and experience on a daily basis and ask why it is so, to explore beyond.

You don't discriminate. By openly examining ideas, beliefs, cultures from around the world, you broaden your own experience. From this elevated level, you now have a position from which you can communicate your ideas and talents to a waiting audience.

From the pulpit, the lectern, the courtroom, the halls of government, or from the privacy of your study, you excite and stimulate those little gray cells into bigger gray cells in the minds of your listeners. You are here to educate the world, to open their minds to broader vistas, to be the example of what they can achieve with the right attitude.

Much like a child lying on the grass on a summer's day creating images out of the puffy clouds floating above in a blue sky, you are here to imagine. Ideas flow with such ease that it seems you just pluck them from the air.

Truly, your reach does extend beyond the present. You are here to lead others to the wondrous world of knowledge, which they will discover in the hallowed rooms of libraries around the world.

Mercury sesquiquintile Saturn:
Your Legacy:
A fine-tooth comb.

Discover Your DNA Treasure:
See that line of stern-looking ancestral portraits lining your hallway, not a hair on their heads out of place? They have their eyes focused on you. You are here to carry on their tradition of recording the Word.

Speaking of hair, you have a brain with a built-in fine-tooth comb. No detail escapes your keen mind and eagle eyes. Your mind combs through information examining every fact with great precision.

By the way, fine-tooth combs date back to 12,500 BCE and have changed little since; it's a perfect image for your thought processes, because hair grows from the head where the brain resides; therefore, hair is a metaphor for your thoughts.

Because you think with great clarity and a fine eye to detail, you are a natural problem-solver. You have the talent to see the bare bones of any project in which you are engaged, and then you proceed to build a lasting structure upon that skeletal outline. You trust the past and live by those established rules if they work; if they don't work, out comes the fine-tooth comb.

Through precision and focus, you reduce a subject to its elements. Like Einstein said: A mathematical equation stands forever. You have an engineer's mind well adapted to architecture, industry, science, and research, and you apply yourself to your work with an economy of effort.

You are the talented architect of thought. You are here to show the world that your work embodies your thoughts, similar to the ancient sketch artists who carved phases of the moon into reindeer bones and pictures of their daily life on cave walls, like the Sumerian scribes who pressed their knowledge into clay tablets, and like the ancient builders who wrote their secret messages within the construction of the temples and churches and stone circles for posterity.

Your talents can also be expressed in the arts. In education, writing and teaching would be based on sound structural components; therefore, you would make a great teacher. Your purpose here is to leave concrete creative accomplishments. They will be deposited in the great libraries of the world, those depositories of knowledge where future generations can "pick your brain."

You are meant to leave behind an enormous fine-tooth comb.

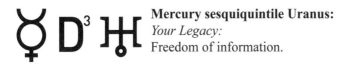

Mercury sesquiquintile Uranus:
Your Legacy:
Freedom of information.

Discover Your DNA Treasure:
Your prehistory is littered with rebellious thinkers who thought not just outside the box but outside the confines of the Earth and reached into the heavens. Your DNA carries global thinking into the future.

You can be sure the first human to carve notches into reindeer bones marking the phases of the moon was one of your ancestors . . . maybe even you in your past life when you sought the secrets of the universe while the rest of the tribe sat around rubbing sticks together wondering what the heck you were doing. You've always thought outside the tribe.

Not always a comfortable position, your mind takes you to places of intellectual freedom and independence. You have the voice of the rebel who speaks out with such intelligence that you mobilize the public consciousness. You know that thoughts are things, that words matter, and you use your words to voice the desire and the human right to live free.

You seek to inform the public. One of the fields in which you would excel is astrology, following in that long line of star gazers who revealed the wonders of the heavens to an amazed world. Flight, escaping the bonds of earth, stirs your being, just as it did for Charles Lindberg, who completed the first solo nonstop flight from New York to Paris in 1927.

Your mind works at a lightning quick pace. While everyone else is thinking A-B-C, you're already at Z. Your thinking zips to accurate conclusions with the speed of light. Flashes of intuition often lead you to accurate insights.

You know that the mind controls the destiny so you may be a proponent of power napping when you take moments out of your eclectic day to drift off to sleep. This allows your subconscious to collect the multiple thoughts darting through your brain. You awake with a start and voila! You have caught the creative light that answers your questions.

The Freedom of Information Act is a legislation you treasure. Regardless of whether your chosen profession is in science, politics, education, or philosophy, you will reside in the halls of memory as one who broke new ground and released tribal thinking into global thinking, one who mentally gave hope to and nourished the soul of intellectual freedom.

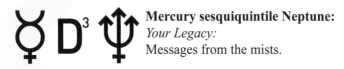

Mercury sesquiquintile Neptune:
Your Legacy:
Messages from the mists.

Discover Your DNA Treasure:

You talk to the flowers and they talk back; you see the world in a droplet of rain water. Your boundless imagination snaps photographs of the images you see in your mind's eye. You are here to manifest your creative potential by humming your lullaby for the world.

Your stream of consciousness flows freely beyond the earthly barriers of time and space as you give voice to the mystical side of life. Your message comes on "little cat feet . . . looking over harbor and city," but rather than moving on, you must express your artistic vision for the world, to lift the spirit of those who seek something beyond the ordinary humdrum of life.

Your dreams are a source of inspiration because they tap into your Akashic records that contain your prehistory. Your inspired message can express through the arts—photography, poetry, fiction—where you spin your magic web.

You are an effective speaker because you are psychically tuned in to the thoughts of others. You know what the audience needs to hear because you sense what they're thinking. On a larger scale, you are tuned in to the shifting mental patterns of society so you are able to incorporate that vision into your creative work.

You may find that the halls of philosophy are the platform from which you preach faith and promise for belief in a better world.

You are sensitive to the harshness in the world; therefore, you require periods of retreat where you can communicate with the hidden world of fantasy. Perhaps you unwind on the silky sands of a tropical island with a cool, fruity drink decorated with paper umbrellas in one hand and a book of romantic verse in the other, where your mind can drift off and swim with the mermaids and float on the moon-beamed waters.

Once renewed, you are back in the world to fulfill your destiny. Your intellect combined with your vast imagination inspires others to follow in your gentle footsteps. Like the Shaolin priest, you leave no footprints on the rice paper, but you do leave a legacy in the public libraries of the world for those who seek the creative mystical side of life.

Mercury sesquiquintile Pluto:
Your Legacy:
Listen to your Mother.

Discover Your DNA Treasure:

You come from a long line of magicians, those who understood the laws of Mother Earth and used those laws to bring about fundamental change and rebirth on this earth. You are here to carry on that tradition in full public view. Cast off your black-hooded cloak, and expose the underbelly of corruption!

You see deep into the needs and desires that motivate human behavior. You stand against attempts to control the media. Your mission is to expose those who seek power over the thoughts of others. You feel this duty deeply and know you must speak these truths in a public forum. Those who would control information had better listen to the Mother.

Your intense intellect manifests in everything you do. You plunge completely into your work. You feed on problems and puzzles. You are the cosmic detective, the researcher, privy to secrets that lay deeply buried. As such, you are the vault of private information and classified secrets, and in this position, you have the power to bring about change in society.

You have the "all-seeing eye" through which you discover the secrets hidden beneath the surface of the physical world. You are able to peer through the microscope into the sub-atomic world that is invisible to human vision.

You are pledged to protect the resources that are necessary for life to continue, whether it is psychological, financial, political, or environmental. Your words resonate as truth down through the ages, even as far as admitting as a child that it was you who cut down the cherry tree.

You are mentally powerful because you have the ability to totally concentrate on your goal like the young mother who, after years of struggle, is the first one in the family to earn a bachelor's degree or the 120-pound mother who lifts a car off her pinned child. You overcome the odds through the power of your mind.

You understand cause and effect especially when it relates to how one thinks. Thoughts are things; thoughts create reality. You are to be here to leave a powerful example of how to use the power of your mind to change the lives of society on fundamental levels. Time to cast your spells.

 **Mercury sesquiquintile Ascendant:**
Your Legacy:
Say it like you see it.

Discover Your DNA Treasure:
Dig up your DNA treasure; solidify your light. Built into your DNA are all those outspoken ancestors urging you to speak your mind. Perhaps they were taught to be seen and not heard, but they're ready to be heard now. You are the chosen one: Say it like you see it.

And you do. You are able to express your views fluently in ways that hold others in your mental embrace. Your delivery flows so naturally that others see you as sincere and somewhat mesmerizing. So, find a stage or podium or soap box, and audiences will gather. The public will identify with your message, for you are the spokesperson in your career, which may be through the arts, publishing, the media, education, politics, or sports -- any platform from which you can speak to a large audience.

Curiously, sometimes you don't even have to speak. Your physical presence alone—the tilt of your eyebrow, your enigmatic smile, the expressive use of your hands and arms—sets you apart from the ordinary speaker. You possess that intangible something that draws people into your sphere. Just your being there invokes speculation and interest.

You are a brand in the sense that others identify you with a "product," an accomplishment. Unlike the simpleminded gardener in the film *Being There,* who has no knowledge of the world, but through a series of circumstances, rises to the top of Washington society where his simple responses to complex questions are taken as pearls of wisdom, your presence is taken seriously because it is based upon pearls of accomplishment.

Highly intelligent, you notice everything around you, which feeds your vast pool of information. You are curious and most likely well read. This coupled with your innate talent of self-expression sets you above the crowd.

Every day when you open your eyes and look through your personal window into the world, you see opportunities to learn from what life has to offer. You approach your day knowing that you will make connections that can impact the collective mind through your chosen profession. Your intelligent curiosity and effortless ability to reach the public consciousness through your given talent will be recorded in the halls of history.

VENUS SPEAKS TO LOVE, BEAUTY, AND JUSTICE

♀ D³ ♂   **Venus sesquiquintile Mars:**
Your Legacy:
Unlock your diary.

Discover Your DNA Treasure:
Not saying that you come from a long line of Casanovas but do keep your ancestors' diaries under wraps. You have inherited a bit of the rascal, and it's now your turn to weave the magic of your dynamic sex appeal to both sexes into something solid for the world to enjoy.

Beyond intimacy, your sense of beauty and flair can whip up a hairstyle that lifts the spirits of a weary woman. Your performance as an entertainer revitalizes the mundane days of the audience.

Your love of new horizons moves and beckons people into the romance of adventure. In your trip around the world in eighty days, you engage people from all walks of life with your refined vitality. You delight in the sensual delights, the tastes and smells of different cultures.

The open acceptance of people in general, and the love and desire for peace and harmony that you project distinguishes you in the eyes of the public.

You have a keen sense of creative balance that serves you well in such professions as sports, literature, the performing arts, music, and politics where your artistic grace and genuine affection for others draws the affection of people. You are in a position to be a role model for what is best in human nature—the desire to have happy relationships, to be creative and productive, to be financially secure, and to enjoy life.

Your audience is waiting for your performance. You are here to use your inherited talents in the venue of your choice. Your creative passion can be expressed quietly behind closed doors or in the big wide open. However you choose to perform, your efforts can have an effect upon the public consciousness.

You should never underestimate what beauty and entertainment can do for the soul of the world. Despair and hopelessness can be lifted and transformed by the acts of one person whose positive creative vitality energizes the listless.

You are here to paint the world with beauty and color. No locks on your diary. It will be stored in the world library for others to read.

♀ D³ ♃   Venus sesquiquintile Jupiter:
Your Legacy:
The love of knowledge.

Discover Your DNA Treasure:

That excellent wine cellar your great-great somebody accumulated over the years stands as testament to your educated taste. With a crystal glass in hand, you relax in a brocade fireside chair in your library surrounded by cherry bookcases filled with volumes on fine art, the collected wisdom of ancient philosophers, and culinary dishes from around the world accompanied by the "Passions" of Joann Sebastian Bach playing in the background.

There's no question you love the finer things in life! You are here to encourage and teach a larger vision of what is best in life. You have a sweeping sense of history, of the romantic, of the connection between cultures. Your love of learning inspires an educated vision of the possibilities for growth in the world. This is the joy you spread to others.

Your warm personality welcomes the world into your embrace. You create a comfortable environment in which you spread your optimism generously with a smile and a helping hand. You are also sympathetic to those who are in need. You feel that society functions best when based upon a strong set of ethics, and your life stands as testimony to that code.

Teaching comes naturally to you, especially in music, the arts, writing, and through higher education, but you are not just a pretty face; although your sense of beauty and proportion brings you recognition through your abilities in the field of the arts—design, color, beauty products, clothing—all the accoutrements that please the senses. You represent the finer things in life.

You experience life's pleasures intimately. You may find that physically traveling the world satisfies your sensual experiences in life, an historical novel and a box of imported dark chocolates tucked in your Kate Spade travel bag.

Through your love of learning, you have a sweeping sense of history, of the romantic, of the connections between people and cultures, which opens the possibilities for growth in this world.

You are here to teach, to open the minds of all people to the wonders of this world. You touch upon the inner desire of those who want to grow beyond their current circumstances. You leave a legacy of the love of knowledge and the joy it bestows.

Venus sesquiquintile Saturn:
Your Legacy:
A blueprint of love.

Discover Your DNA Treasure:
You come from a prehistory of stone builders who put their hearts into what they constructed. Think the Great Pyramids, the Sphinx, Stonehenge, and the Chartres Cathedral. Time, patience, and artistry have combined in your DNA history.

You have the patience of Job—not Steve Jobs—rather the Biblical one, pronounced *J-oh-b*. Your self-discipline and endurance in pursuit of your goals sets you apart from those who want a quick fix. You know that things take time and you are in for the long haul. You approach your goal with patience and a serious attitude. You're most willing to spend long hours pursuing the balanced elegance you seek.

You take full responsibility for the job you perform, carrying more than your load because you want the job done right. Like the ant who, against all the laws of weight distribution, carries fifty to one hundred times its own weight, and has a specific task in the colony, and whose movements pollinate, disperse seeds, and move soil to circulate nutrients that breathe life into many ecosystems, your endurance and self-discipline through creative avenues contributes to the consciousness of society.

You set guidelines through a well-planned blueprint. You feel comfortable with the enclosures you have created, a place where you can build your creative structures and not waste time on embellishments that detract from the simple lines of beauty. Your love of structure is seen through a disciplined eye.

You add to the world's knowledge through your creative work. Your knowledge can be spread through writing, speaking, and teaching, through the arts such as sculpting, through the entertainment and sports fields, through your financial and business acumen, or through your scientific and mathematical abilities. However, your contribution teaches that all these expressions have one thing in common: They encompass both beauty and functionality.

You have a serious side, an aura of reserve that people warm up to once they appreciate the talent and dedication you have put into your achievements. You see beauty in justice and the laws that bind society into a healthy functioning whole. Your legacy is functional beauty.

Against all odds, you can "move the rubber tree plant."

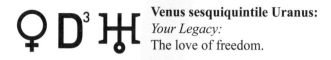

Venus sesquiquintile Uranus:
Your Legacy:
The love of freedom.

Discover Your DNA Treasure:
Someone you know was there at the signing of the Declaration of Independence and the sewing of the USA original flag. Look closely at the paintings, and you'll see a resemblance.

Your inborn love of freedom is in your blood and well expressed in the phrase: "Life, Liberty, and the pursuit of Happiness." These are not just flowery words to you; this phrase is the declaration you live by.

You embrace life with spontaneity, looking for the unusual, the people and projects that fulfill your desire for excitement and lift your relationships out of the "normal." Heaven forbid you have normal relationships! How boring!

Your mantra may well be: "Let there be spaces in your togetherness." You believe in relationships that allow each individual to express their values freely.

Your extremely unusual creative abilities have an appeal that entices the public; they are curious about what makes you tick. In the performing arts, you startle, surprise, and create excitement; you provide that jolt of electricity that makes life vibrant and alive. Even though at times your behavior seems outrageous, drawing social *tsk-tsking* from the more conservative elements in society, you don't care. You know that underneath all the posturing, they would love to be able to express their repressed needs.

You attract the good things in life, which can include wealth. You pour your resources—life and limb, comfort and security—into projects that reach beyond the expectations of a settled society. Your joy lies in breaking earthly bonds and soaring high above in a more rarified atmosphere.

In your world, beauty, harmony, and balance extend beyond the art of personal relationships. You look beyond the interconnections of personal lives into the harmonic world of nature and find pleasure in discovering new connections. Your discoveries stimulate the general public, enlarging their vision of what can be. Your futuristic visions leave a lasting impact upon the public consciousness.

You are here to solidify your unique accomplishments that prove to others that there is a place for them where they can experience "Life, Liberty, and the pursuit of Happiness."

Venus sesquiquintile Neptune:
Your Legacy:
The healing power of love.

Discover Your DNA Treasure:

Feel the tidal pull to cloistered spaces? Rightly so, because you are connected to the romantic mystics of the past, "feeling out of sight for the ends of being and ideal grace." Your extreme sensitivity feeds your vast imagination. You are emotionally and psychically tuned to the eternal rhythms of life, shown by the tide that washes ashore and then returns gently to the sea on a daily basis. Natures' message of balance between the yin and the yang is there for all to see. Some look but do not see; you look and feel the rhythm deep within you.

A daily stroll along the seashore or lakeside where you can feel the water tickle your toes and flow over your feet lifts your soul. During an early morning walk through the fog when shadows smudge the physical world around you, your creative vision allows a peek into the mystical world of little forest creatures, sprites, and fairies.

Your psychic ability is so pronounced that you may need periods of seclusion to shed any negative emotions you absorb in your daily life. Therefore, you need to attend retreats or places of spiritual quiet where you can meditate and replenish. From this place, your love of the beauty found in the gentle harmony of refined music, poetry, and literature finds an expression that transcends the ordinary.

You have deep sympathy for the suffering in the world. Your calm magnetic personality, your physical presence, has a pronounced effect that people respond to. Your presence, your touch, your soothing words have a healing effect upon those in need of physical or spiritual grace. You embody the mystical healing power of love.

Even if you are involved in the business world, your gentility and kindness shines through in your treatment of others. And your vast imagination is an asset in all your endeavors.

You are here to manifest the light from another world. Perhaps you have lived in that world in your prehistory; it's in your DNA, and now the thirst of the public consciousness calls for your talents. You are called to contribute your talent to the cosmic library so that others who follow in your footsteps may find joy in the hidden mystical world.

Perhaps you spray a fine lavender mist on your pillow each night to ease you gently into your dream world.

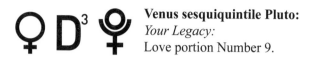

Venus sesquiquintile Pluto:
Your Legacy:
Love portion Number 9.

Discover Your DNA Treasure:

In a past life, you were the magician concocting "Love Potion Number 9," that magical elixir that opened the door to deep abiding love relationships. Nine is the whole ball of wax, and you want it all. Somebody in your lineage most likely wrote the marriage vow "'til death do us part."

That intense love still abides deep inside you. Your emotions are powerful; therefore, whatever you focus on has your undivided attention. You are totally committed to and understand the transforming power of love. Certainly your commitment to that "one" person is part of your deep desire to find complete bonding with your soul mate. Roses on the pillow each night?

However, that deep compulsion translates into everything you do in life. As Steve Jobs said: "The only way to do great work is to love what you do." Your love is intense and will overcome the odds.

You are the iron fist in the velvet glove because you can accomplish your goals through the use of diplomacy. You have a powerful magnetism that fascinates the public; they see in you a mix of refinement and romanticism and an indomitable will to succeed.

Built into your DNA is a heritage of do-or-die individuals like the British suffragette, Emmeline Pankhurst, named by *Time* as one of the most important people of the twentieth century who shook society through her love of justice by helping women gain the right to vote.

Nothing stands in your way. You challenge preconceived ideas of what pleasures should be allowed in society and often send your detractors "down the rabbit hole" looking for an out. You exemplify the person "who will never be beaten."

In this lifetime, you know it's time to make your mark in society. You could apply yourself to the written word to the point of exhaustion, to a sport where you train your body to do what seems impossible, to a political cause that changes the body politic, or to the pursuit of a business enterprise that garners great wealth—but always with an eye to equality.

Ultimately, you understand the moral obligation that your personal power demands from you. You use the rewards you have received from your victories to transform the global mind through love, justice, and equality.

♀ D³ ASC
Venus sesquiquintile Ascendant:
Your Legacy:
Prayer in the morning.

Discover Your DNA Treasure:
Your long forgotten ancestor most likely inscribed on the walls of an Egyptian tomb this prayer to the morning: "O Ra, you giver of all life. The Earth rejoices when it sees your golden rays . . . to behold your beauties every day."

Perhaps that is why you chant that mantra as you look through your window each morning. What you see is a world hungry for love, harmony, balance, and beauty. You are empowered by this view, which is expressed through your chosen path in this life.

"Your face is your case." In the most positive sense, this one quip from the Seinfeld series speaks to the aura of your personal appearance. Your physical presence makes a statement that draws others into your world. Your body, your mannerisms, the grace with which you express yourself is magnetic.

You are the notable figure with a big smile and welcoming hug whose persona exemplifies open acceptance and happiness. People feel comfortable and ease in your presence. As such, you are the perfect spokesperson for an idea, a cause, or a product that enhances the pleasures that life has to offer.

Your popularity could support a life in politics, public service, or arbitration, because you treat relationships with diplomacy, tactfulness, and a refined touch. Your position at the table assures fairness. You are the ambassador of good will.

Your athletic grace can excel in the field of sports where you give hours of pleasure to those who watch your performances. The arts may be your calling where your creative eye for design pleases the eye of the beholder. Through creative writing, your words flow with stories of personal relationships and the power of love. Through the media your words take on significant meanings.

As you awake to the chirping of the early morning birds, you are reminded you are here to awaken the consciousness of the public through your ability to paint a picture from a template of peace, enjoyment, and the pleasures of life.

When John Lennon was in school, he was asked what he waned to be when he grew up. He wrote, "Happy!" He was told he didn't understand the assignment. He told them they didn't understand life. Lennon's your kind of guy.

MARS SPEAKS TO THE ACTION PRINCIPLE

♂ D³ ♃

Mars sesquiquintile Jupiter:
Your Legacy:
Push the limits of exploration.

Discover Your DNA Treasure:
Kahlil Gibran wrote: "A little knowledge that acts is worth infinitely more than much knowledge that is idle." You are a seeker. Whether you traveled with the mountain men who opened the Oregon Trail or you lived it vicariously through the Pulitzer Prize-winning novel *The Way West*, you have a thirst for adventure and the exploration of unknown territories.

You are the pioneer on new pathways of knowledge, a fighter for the space to grow. The first to volunteer for a new journey, you put yourself out there to shine your light on the land of new experiences that increase awareness. Your exploits may be registered in the annals of history.

You have a driving desire to extend beyond, to break the existing record, to be best at what you do, surpassing all others like Jimmy Guthrie with his nineteen motorcycle Grand Prix wins, or like a young Mozart whose intensity and creative energy pushed him to compose his first work at age five.

That itch you have is caused by wondering what else is out there. No amount of scratching will ease that discomfort; it requires action. You already know what you need to do. It's built into your DNA, fueled by your lineage.

Your actions tap into the mind of society, probing and prodding, pushing others to explore new territory in which to spread their wings. Yours is not a gentle hand but rather one that grabs hold of the wheel and, by your actions, dares others to follow, to take action on their own, to loosen the ties that bind them to a limited past.

You are here to be recognized in history as the individual with drive and passion, the one who is always reaching, the one who seeks the limits of what is possible. You are the teacher, the example of courage, and the desire to completely immerse yourself in the lust for life.

From an unknown source: "Someone once told me not to bite off more than I could chew. I told them I would rather choke on greatness than nibble on mediocrity!" That must have been you!

♂ D³ ♄   **Mars sesquiquintile Saturn:**
Your Legacy:
Move the world.

Discover Your DNA Treasure:

For some reason your parents named you Archie, most likely short for Archimedes. Check your birth certificate. Archimedes (281 BCE), one of the greatest mathematicians and engineers in world history, wrote: "Give me a lever long enough and a fulcrum on which to place it, and I shall move the world."

This kind of lineage should straighten your spine and make you sit up and take notice. You don't need prodding, however, because you use every ounce of your energy to accomplish your goals. You're patient; you plan carefully and seldom miss the essential components of any endeavor. You are the efficiency expert and organizational planner.

You understand how things are put together, but you enjoy taking them apart to discover how they work. You examine the skeletal outline of a problem to determine any cracks or weaknesses in the structure. Like the bees who build their hives in hexagonal cells, you too make the most efficient use of space.

Rules are important because they define the limits within which you work. They provide the outline, the perimeters, the foundation upon which the world is constructed. The legal profession, law enforcement, and the military are built upon the necessity for rules for a stable society.

You understand and are comfortable with discipline and precision; however, you will examine the rules to see if there are any flaws. You may suddenly exclaim, "Eureka! I have found it!" Then you set about to change the rules to create a more practical approach to order in your universe.

You are the perfect teacher, patient and calm, taking the student one step at a time through the learning process. You could be noted for the managerial care of a business or the Earth, a captain in industry, or an educational leader. As Plato voiced in the Republic, "Only the benevolent can be depended upon to steer and hold steady the ship of state." You are that steady hand.

Your keen sense of timing is exceptional, so you understand that now is the time to shine your creative light upon the strong foundations you represent and prove that you have a long enough lever to move through the world.

Go, Archie!

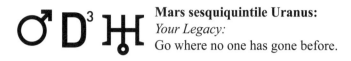

Mars sesquiquintile Uranus:
Your Legacy:
Go where no one has gone before.

Discover Your DNA Treasure:
You are an original; you dance to an off-beat melody. Just like your wild and crazy ancestors (we won't ask what you did in your past lives with those explosions and rockets), you are not hemmed in by the past or the present; your focused beam is on the future. You cannot be defined. "Definitions belong to the definers, not the defined" (Toni Morrison).

No nine-to-five job for you. You need the freedom to explore the cosmos on your own. You need that space for your creativity to flourish. You are here to stand as an example of what freedom to act means, to let the world know in clear outspoken terms that "your real job . . . is to free somebody else. This is not just a grab-bag candy game" (Morrison).

You're well energized in that journey, because you have a limitless energy supply, a rechargeable battery. Words are liberating; you also show by your actions the necessity of fighting for your inalienable right to space on this planet. What you accomplish lifts the desire for creative exploration in those that follow.

You break the established laws of a limited society, projecting through the atmospheric haze of the public mind like a rocket breaking through the stratosphere into the exosphere, that place of free-moving particles.

And you are a "moving particle." Super-charged, you find boring more than boring; you find it stultifying! Big word that means: tedious and restrictive routines that destroy enthusiasm and initiative. And you will have none of that.

You are in a constant state of excitement that excites the interest of others in fields outside the normal bounds of societal thinking; you go places that others may consider taboo. Your inventive approach to challenging thoughts unsettles the status quo. But that is your job. You are here to break the earthly bonds, to reach for something beyond, to explore beyond the limits, to be the example honored in the universal libraries as the one to follow if you dare.

As astronaut Ron Garan said, "We are limited only by our imagination and our will to act."

Don your flight suit; break the barriers!

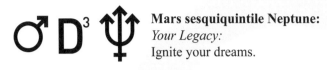

Mars sesquiquintile Neptune:
Your Legacy:
Ignite your dreams.

Discover Your DNA Treasure:

You have a psychic awareness of the unseen world around you along with a desire to direct your energy into the mystical and healing realms. Unlike the romantic image of the Lady of Shallot who drifts tragically upon a flowing stream toward a doomed fate, you direct the course of your boat. You have a steady hand upon the oar and a destination in mind.

In addition, you are tuned in to any dangers that glide beneath the surface so you have the ability to maneuver around obstacles to reach your goals. Your physical grace can be expressed in body movement where you seem to float above the laws of gravity.

Folklore has it that the seventh son of the seventh son, with no females in between, has special powers. Actually, the reverse is true; this is a case of copying the feminine magic. Your DNA carries the seventh of the seventh tradition into this life. This gifts you as a healer, the witch who has the charms to cure the ailments of this world by using the powers inherited at birth.

You are driven to help those in need, and your abilities may find a home in social programs, the law, psychotherapy, and the healing arts. You are especially tuned in to dreams.

You may also choose to direct your creative talents to the world of fantasy and imagination. You could capture the elusive world of imagination through creative writing, photography, cinema, music, and dance.

Speaking of dancing, was that you floating under the powerful new moon as your coven cast magical spells of healing and abundance over the Earth? Of course it was! Your reach binds the Earth to the Heaven.

You desire to reach "beyond the boundaries of life, to the depth and breadth and height your soul can reach when feeling out of sight for the ends of being and ideal grace" (E. B. Browning).

Your mission in this life is to reveal your mystical abilities to the public, to lead them through the physical fog of the three-dimensional world into those mist-shrouded shores of the eternal sea where faith abides, where dreams are real, and where the Sun will rise again.

 **Mars sesquiquintile Pluto:**
Your Legacy:
Charge the hill.

Discover Your DNA Treasure:
"Far better is it to dare mighty things . . . though checkered by failure . . . than to live in a gray twilight that knows not victory nor defeat." Like the great Teddy Roosevelt, you have dared mighty things and now you're back in this life to make an impact. Maybe you'll even get a teddy bear named after you. Of course, you'll have to save the bear cub to do so.

Your exploits are bigger than life; you will defy the odds. You ride roughly up the hill to overcome the biggest challenges to achieve your goal. With great courage and intensity, you will overcome.

You have the power to transform society at fundamental levels. Against seemingly overwhelming odds, you will fight to the end defending your sense of justice and more often than not, you will win. And if you don't, you will try again.

Your bold feats are legendary. The public asks who was that Wonder Woman? . . . that person who mass-produced a moving machine; the individual who overcame misogyny and gained the women's right to vote; the bard from Strafford-upon-Avon who wrote plays about political power grabs, struggles with social conformity, and sexual identity. They all overcame the odds and changed cultures.

Because you have an internal GPR (ground penetrating radar), you see into the forces that lie beneath the visible world. You may be drawn to the physical world of science where things can be measured and quantified or the world of business and finance. But then again, you may prefer the metaphysical world that explores what exists beyond what is seen by the naked eye.

You have the courage to support the things you believe in, to cast off the witch's cloak of invisibility and come out from behind the scenes to work your magic. Like the three witches in *MacBeth* who chant "Double, double toil and trouble, fire burns and cauldron bubble, scale of dragon, tooth of wolf" you are not one to be trifled with.

Use your plutonian energy pack that never seems to run out of power to transform some segment of society. Charge the hill of ignorance and plant the flag of victory at the top. You light the spark of courage to make fundamental change in those who follow.

♂ **D³ ASC** **Mars sesquiquintile Ascendant:**
Your Legacy:
Do it your way.

Discover Your DNA Treasure:
You bring the spirit of individualism into this life. You approach every day with energy and enthusiasm, spurred by the inherited desire to explore, investigate, and probe the nature of life.

Like the surf men of old who jumped into row boats during wild storms in the icy Atlantic, risking their own lives to save mariners in distress, you jump into action in whatever you do. You thrive on the adrenaline rush, so taking chances is built into your DNA.

There's a competitive nature in you that is determined to overcome any physical restraints. You express yourself directly and in your own unique manner, sometimes through both your physical stamina and your verbal skills. You have the style and speed to "float like a butterfly, but sting like a bee," as said by famous boxer Muhammad Ali. In certain circumstances, you could use that determination to overcome physical challenges.

Your strength and competitive outlook instills confidence in your abilities to overcome challenges. Sports is one outlet where your energy can find a positive outlet or you may travel around the globe to participate in dangerous adventures or you may overcome what some would deem debilitating physical challenges.

Your verbal skills can be showcased in your ability to write sweeping stories about individualism and the right to choose one's own path, stories about rising up and taking action against those who would stifle your free spirit. These stories appeal to any culture anywhere—the right to make one's own path in life.

You have a sensual spark that draws the interests of others. In any profession, you add that energetic lively and sometimes challenging aspect to what you do.

No one fights your battles for you, however; you want to be personally involved. You live in the moment and are quick to respond to cultural shifts in society and may even be part of the movements.

You are here to stir up the individualist spirit in society, to leave behind your unique signature as representative of one who fights for the right to believe and live freely. No matter the culture, your individualist qualities speak a universal language.

JUPITER SPEAKS TO GROWTH, OPTIMISM, AND KNOWLEDGE

♃ D³ ♄ **Jupiter sesquiquintile Saturn:**
Your Legacy:
Balance the seesaw.

Discover Your DNA Treasure:
You come from a history of philosophical tight-rope walkers, those people who disciplined their thought processes to maintain a balance between expansion and conservatism. As the larger-than-life figure Winston Churchill wrote: "The inherent vice of capitalism is the unequal sharing of blessings: The inherent virtue of socialism is the equal sharing of miseries." He understood the difficulty of maintaining a balance between unlimited expansion and the restriction of growth.

You, however, are a responsible conservative individual with an optimistic streak. Built into your DNA is a faith in the future that is based upon a well-planned common-sense approach. You have that stability and commanding presence that inspires trust from the public.

You know how to formulate your ethics and morality into a message that stimulates the public consciousness. You push the envelope just so far then build a safe structure to maintain that progress. You persist at this growth-by-inches approach because you want to ensure that your message will contribute to the universal pool of knowledge, a legacy for future generations.

You use time wisely, concentrating on issues that you find important. Your focus could be in business, the legal profession, government, education, or religion where your ethics and optimism play a part in stabilizing society. Through the literary arts, you tell of the struggles between faith and despair with the goal of illuminating the principles of freedom over restrictive societal rules.

The message you are to leave this lifetime is a question and a statement. You want to climb that mountain? Make sure you have the ropes and pitons and safety harness. You want to write that book? Make sure you have a well-planned outline. You want to bring positive social change? Make sure you have supporters backing up your cause. You want to create music? Know the scales. The message is that if you want to succeed, back up your vision with knowledge.

You have the creative talent to stand in the annals of history as an individual who lived by a set of rules that allowed faith in one's vision of what is possible through belief in growth based upon preparation.

♃ D³ ♅

Jupiter sesquiquintile Uranus:
Your Legacy:
The sky's the limit . . . and even beyond.

Discover Your DNA Treasure:
People may think you're lucky but if one goes back far enough, luck becomes inevitable. And your DNA traces a long way back. You come from a time of dreamers and inventors, those who thought big and beyond the limits, unfettered by the restrictions imposed upon them by an obedient society.

Behind your baby blues (choose your color) vibrates a huge questioning mind fissured with a network of tiny wrinkles. More wrinkles, more working brain power.

Why not? How come? What if? Who says? In your prehistory, you most likely wore out your parents, teachers, friends, coworkers, employers, and probably the clerk at the local grain and smithy shop with your endless questions. Through that eternal search for answers, through that thirst for knowledge, you have arrived at a pinnacle where you now must showcase your talent.

"You build it and they will come" is no longer a fantasy line from a film (*Field of Dreams*). Now is the time for you to build it because they will come around. Your intuitive flashes of insight coupled with the faith you have in your amazing creative abilities startle and amaze a sleeping public mind. The breadth of your knowledge and your ingenious solutions to problems often stuns others who wonder who that crazy person is, perhaps realizing you're not so crazy after all when your solutions prove their worth.

You represent the idea that personal freedom is essential if we are to allow the creative seeds of each generation to take root and grow. You may travel the world by trains, planes, and automobiles but you prefer the open skies, perhaps by hot air balloon? Or jet? Or spaceship?

The sky is no limit, just a beckoning come hither. You can startle the public through your artistic abilities that break traditional lines or through messages that break old stereotypes about social conditions. Your legacy to the world is the concept of liberty and freedom in which one is able to express her unique very individualistic creative talent.

Free from the gray shades of the mental palettes of the naysayers, you paint the world in broad vibrant color!

♃ D³ ⚴♆ Jupiter sesquiquintile Neptune:
Your Legacy:
The link between worlds.

Discover Your DNA Treasure:

You are a mystic, a poet, an empathic, who feels more than thinks. The sensitive nature of your DNA prehistory has flowed from a stream of consciousness through the ages into a vast ocean of psychic awareness. You now embody this talent and you are here to baptize others through your compassionate and spiritual sensitivity.

You are the connector, the link between this world and the next. You have stood in that mist shrouded world in the past. Now you must, through your immersion in society, teach others that faith in what cannot be seen but is nevertheless felt is as real as the physical world of matter. You may find that you need to introduce others to the world of mystical arts.

A great joy comes from ministering to the needy, the underprivileged, and the sick in mind, body, and spirit. You reach out through your work with social programs to ensure that laws are made to protect the health and welfare of society. Your generous spirit opens doorways to the halls of justice and to the hearts of those who reside therein.

Not content to retreat to cloistered halls, your mission is to be seen and heard. You may use your creative gifts through literature that lifts the soul or through transmitting messages between this world and the spirit world or through religious music or through mystical films depicting faith above reason.

You may represent a philosophical movement that is a beacon of freedom that dispels the fog of public indifference. You dream of a world where a "house is not divided against itself" but is whole and happy.

Your enormous creative potential now becomes an asset to offer to the world. You feel the magic in the mist, in the poetry of life. Your strength comes from your gentleness, your silent voice that often speaks louder than those who shout from the rooftops.

You are a healer on many levels, in whatever profession you choose. You understand that "nothing happens unless first we dream." You are here to make your dreams of a gentler more compassionate world a reality in the halls of memory.

♃ D³ ♇   **Jupiter sesquiquintile Pluto:**
Your Legacy:
Faith moves mountains.

Discover Your DNA Treasure:

Look deep into your past and you may find a line of witches and wizards, those ancestors who worked their magic, spinning straw into gold. Perhaps you were one of them. You came into this life with incredible strength that you are here to use to transform a cause. Physical size does not matter, for contained within you is the will to work your magic.

No longer hidden because of condemnation by religious authorities or public ignorance, you step into the light and proclaim your power for the enlightenment of society.

You might, at the age of eighty-eight, begin a two-year journey on a 3,200 mile walk across a country to advocate for campaign finance or you could, as a young pilot, be credited with twenty-two aerial victories, four shared, and six possibles, fighting an evil enemy. Whatever path you take, your heroic actions inspire countless people to look to the future with faith and hope that the future can change for the better.

You have the power to focus your will so intensely that you can move mountains. Case in point: A tiny wiggly worm, tough and resistant, has the power to transform a mountain of cast-off food scraps into nutrient rich compost—you might say it can turn garbage into gold.

Your efforts can be directed to transforming the environment, working hand-in-hand with the laws of nature, to uncover the mysteries of Mother Earth. Then, with trowel in hand, you're off to teach the world how to regenerate and grow.

The original environmentalists were ancient farmers around the world who knew how to rotate their crops and nourish the land in accordance with the rhythms of nature. They transformed the land for a more abundant harvest.

You have insight into the fundamental underpinnings of life, and your passion can be expressed in a number of professions. You are here to contribute your intense talents through art and music, through the practice of the magical arts, through political change, or through your chosen faith, all of which will resonate deep within the public breast.

♃ D³ ASC

Jupiter sesquiquintile Ascendant:
Your Legacy:
Faith in yourself.

Discover Your DNA Treasure:

He drew a cartoon mouse, and his art was rejected; she was mocked because of her appearance; he was the gangly 199th pick in the sixth round of a sports team, but these people never gave up. They went on to become the head of a multi-billion-dollar entertainment company, the "first lady of the world," and one of the greatest sports figures in history.

Like them, your signature is your self-confidence, enthusiasm, and optimistic look at life. You see the glass not half-full but rather brimming over the top. Self-achievement is built into your DNA. You are here to encourage people to succeed on a grand scale by your personal example.

Your creative vision appeals to people around the globe. You dare to dream and make those dreams a reality. No mountain is too high for you to climb because you have faith in yourself. Every morning, you look through a window where the vistas are clear and beckoning. Your "visions of sugar plums" don't just dance in your head, you're here to set them on the table.

Your body is a temple that you honor because you know that your physical presence influences all age groups around the world. What they see is someone who cares enough about themselves and what they represent to maintain the grounds.

Because of your reputation and stature, you can influence legislation that protects those under represented segments of the population. You are the poster "child" whose image evokes dreams of what others can be. The public looks at you with eyes full of wonder.

Sometimes just being there makes a statement even if you don't speak. You carry an aura of good will that speaks to the public. They sense the sincerity with which you engage life.

Underlying your message is a basic decency and ethic that resonates in all you do. Behind all the parades and pageantry, in front of the spotlights, there is an essential you that stands for honesty and faith in the bounty of life.

You will go down in history as an example of someone who has a deep emotional commitment to excellence, a person with a clear vision filled with hope buoyed by an ethical life well lived.

SATURN SPEAKS TO
RESPONSIBILITY AND LIMITS

♄ D³ ♅

Saturn sesquiquintile Uranus:
Your Legacy:
Discovery through discipline.

Discover Your DNA Treasure:
Your ancestral DNA is populated with those Archimedes types who exclaim, "Eureka! I have found it!" You stand for those individuals who, after long periods of investigation, find a brilliant solution to a long examined problem.

You break the mold. One might say you're a cautious rebel. You are the genius who, from several principles and a well-structured platform, breaks those rules that no longer apply.

Even though your ideas, your approach, and your work may initially seem unusual or out of bounds, eventually it's recognized as based upon a thoroughly researched system. You show others that preparation can launch them way beyond the mainstream of thought where they startle others with a show of fireworks.

Your creative talent may find a home in math, science, engineering, astrology, and other metaphysical subjects that are based upon long-held sets of rules that can be the springboard for intuitive discoveries.

Your understanding of the mechanics of the human body and how its parts function may take you into sports where you intuitively know how to move your body according to the laws of physics, and sometimes you seem to break those laws. You have the body and mind control of a Shaolin priest.

You have intuitive insight into the public mind and you can anticipate the trends of those thought patterns. You break through the resistance of conservative serious attitudes and put a little pizzazz in the punch. Because you have insight into human behavior, your thoughtful, calm approach often draws out surprising revelations from individuals. The media may draw upon your talents. The public sees you as different but also dependable and thoughtful. You carry yourself with a sense of dignity and reserve, then, out of the blue, you surprise them with that touch of quirky behavior.

Your patient hours of training result in amazing feats of accomplishment. You stand in the halls of cosmic memory as a disciplined rebel, beckoning those who follow to do the same.

Saturn sesquiquintile Neptune:
Your Legacy:
Fairy tales come true.

Discover Your DNA Treasure:
You know things, secret things. The secrets of mystical societies passed down through your DNA where rituals empowered knowledge is now yours to demonstrate. You are here to step through that gauzy curtain onto the stage and into the public limelight where the world will benefit from what you can do.

Your enormous creativity is now focused in this life for all the world to see. You still need cloistered caverns from which to work, time alone to work with the psychic visions that come to you when you are released from the physical restraints of daily life. It is here in your dream world that the music of the spheres plays for you.

In literature, filmmaking, photography, and mystical studies, you work with the abstract and you have the advantage of creating something solid from your limitless imagination for the benefit of the world. You notice and give expression to the subtleties of life; not much gets by you. Your abilities are supported by your foresight and organizational planning.

You build upon tradition, using the fences of the past to contain and give form to your fantasies where the spiritual world of imagination and wisdom play, where angels are real and fairies and mermaids exist, where compassion is shown through the gentle touch of strong healing hands.

Because you have one foot in the physical world and the other in the spiritual world, you feel a responsibility for the human condition. You have insight into the secret forces that would undermine support for the needy. Your sense of honor and duty dictate that you take a leadership role to impress upon society their duty to take care of the least among us.

Your vast storehouse of knowledge coupled with your ability to perceive things in the future, beyond the normal use of the five senses, aids you in finding solutions that seem beyond the current mind set. You are the embodiment of the spiritual gifts of creative imagination and compassion, which manifests in practical practice in this world. You are here to prove that, "Yes, Virginia, there is a Santa Claus."

You have one foot in the "real" world and the other foot in a fairy tale. And that's just fine with you. You combine the best of both worlds.

 **Saturn sesquiquintile Pluto:**
Your Legacy:
Magicians may apply; experience needed.

Discover Your DNA Treasure:
"Double, double toil and trouble: Fire burn, and cauldron bubble" (Shakespeare). You have distant memories of those dire warnings chanted around a boiling cauldron in a dark cave while thunder rolled across the heavens; however, you no longer fear toil and trouble. And you don't need "Eye of newt and toe of frog" to work your magic.

Not saying that you wouldn't resort to that, but you have other methods to employ today. You understand your responsibility in bringing about fundamental change in institutions that control the welfare of society.

You now have the power to identify and then change what seems immovable and entrenched.

You move in circles where the world is within your power to change. You have a deep understanding of the laws by which life operates. Your organizational thought process and your ability to apply your mind to practical matters finds you in places where you influence large segments of society.

Maybe it's those laser-beam eyes that focus so intensely on a mission that others feel hypnotized by your ability to achieve. You could be a captain of industry or involved in the heady world of finance where your reserved but deeply felt passions change the landscape. You can accomplish what others think impossible.

You open the world mind to knowledge that was previously in the hands of a few who operated behind the scenes. You give voice to hidden truths. Whether you search the depths of space or the expanse of global communication, or express through your art or political cause, you want the truth. Your intensity shows in the strong stances you take.

Exposing truth does give you permission to dance naked and with abandon under the full moon; however, you would choose to perform those traditional rituals fully robed. There is dignity to consider.

However you work your magic, you are here to be the responsible instrument who shines the public consciousness upon the need for fundamental resources to support and sustain a secure society.

Witches and wizards may apply.

♄ D³ ASC

Saturn sesquiquintile Ascendant:
Your Legacy:
Make hay while the sun shines.

Discover Your DNA Treasure:
From your ancestral timekeepers who kept the sun dials clean and properly aligned to those who oiled the clocks of the great cathedrals, your DNA history is replete with an awareness of the value of time.

You realize that timing is everything, that when an opportunity arises, you must act before that opportunity expires. Mother Time waits for no one. Therefore, you respect time and sense its limitations. You stand upon your past, live in the present, and prepare for the future. Your journey may be solitary where you stand alone and test yourself against the elements. You may be *In Search of Lost Time*, believed by some as one of the most respected novels of the twentieth century.

Focused, you would rather "sing one song than interpret the thousand" (Jack London). You live your life on your own terms, simplified and stripped of the useless accoutrements that society often proffers. You prefer to create your own unique vision, to look through your personal window at the world in uncluttered terms, uninfluenced by what other landscapers have left behind. You see beauty in simplicity. You are here to give that message to the world.

You realize that your creative talents must be put to good use. Not willing or not able to rely upon the assistance of others, you carve your own path. You don't expect success to come easily. True success for you is the old Horatio Alger theme—young person with no support succeeds through self reliance, an eagerness to learn, and a powerful sense of justice.

Not deterred by rejection, you continue to work at climbing the ladder of success, encouraged by your daily vision of what you can be.

You work hard to be true to your principles, thereby gaining the respect of society. Once there, you feel obligated to spearhead organizations that lend support to those who struggle against all odds to achieve through their particular talents. You are here to show the world and to be remembered for the truth that through hard work and perseverance, you can bloom in adversity.

Grab your pitchfork!

URANUS SPEAKS TO INDIVIDUALITY AND FREEDOM

Uranus sesquiquintile Neptune:
Your Peer Group Legacy:
Awaken compassion.

Discover Your Peer Groups' DNA treasure:
You, in the sense of your peer group, are willing to take risks and challenge the imagination, the social responsibilities, and the spiritual concepts of your times. You demand the right to intellectual freedom, the right to express your enormous talents and your spiritual beliefs in the way you see fit. You are willing to work with others to achieve these goals.

You carve new pathways into the future. Your purpose is to lift the public consciousness to a higher plane of understanding, to teach them to look forward toward a freer future. This purpose can be achieved through awakening ancient philosophies that now need to be exposed to future generations. It's time to shine the light on astrology, the hidden truths in the Tarot deck, clairvoyance, magic, and mystery. You may join and work with metaphysical groups to enlighten the public consciousness.

You can inspire the world with your unique creative abilities because of your desire to share the joy you experience when in the throes of artistic inspiration. In music, you "smell the sea and feel the sky . . . and let your soul and spirit fly into the mystic" (Van Morrison). Your prose could be described as "inherently mystical."

Those same feelings are invoked when you seek to liberate the suffering of the less fortunate. Until you "extend the circle of compassion to all living things, you will not find peace" (Albert Schweitzer). After your immersion in the effort to help humanity, you may find that the "two means of refuge from the miseries of life are music and cats." Both create rhythms that soothe the soul (Schweitzer).

You teach others independence of mind through higher ideals, and you influence public opinion through your off-beaten pathways towards a universal ideal. Your peer group leaves a legacy of those whose free flights of imagination into ethereal realms have enlightened the social consciousness of the world.

Uranus sesquiquintile Pluto:
Your Peer Group Legacy:
Progress upon the ashes.

Discover Your Peer Group's DNA Treasure:
Your peer group has the insight to recognize when the foundation is crumbling. Built upon a deep emotional need to be free from the restrictive rules governing politics, religion, and finances, and to expose and enlighten society about sexual behavior and the fundamental processes of birth and death, your peer group rises up and speaks out. Like David overcoming Goliath, individual acts of rebellion, the casting of a small stone, bring down the mighty monsters that loom over society.

You no longer bow down to those who try to dominate and control the psychological welfare and necessary resources of others. Society is ready for a revolutionary mind reset. Your peer group will push all the right buttons through your chosen professions.

Sexual mores undergo transformation as shown by the liberating of women from the restraints of the corset and living openly in a mansion in pajamas surrounded by willing bunnies. Shocking events in your day.

The economy needs a major overhaul. Revolutionary programs that put workers back to rebuilding the crumbling infrastructure of a country along with rebuilding their financial security through jobs transforms the working class.

The restrictive laws that govern society are under assault. Standing up to a system that allows crimes against minorities to go unpunished gives voice to spiritually motivated human rights activists.

From groundbreaking thoughts on the meaning of life's transitions pioneered by works such as the five stages of grief, through a cubist's dramatic portrayal of a war-time bombing, your efforts at breaking the old ways of looking at life transform the world's rigid view of life's processes.

Your peer group will not tolerate any accepted tradition that blocks the road to social progress. You refuse to obey the laws of established authority when those laws impede personal freedom. Your generation represents those who take up the pitchfork against the cannon and somehow overcome the odds.

♅ D³ ASC

Uranus sesquiquintile Ascendant:
Your Legacy:
The open window.

Discover Your DNA Treasure:
From the blasphemous *On the Revolution of the Heavenly Spheres,* in 1543, which postulated that the Earth was not the center of the universe, to the tumultuous obscenity trial in 1960 of *Lady Chatterly's Lover*, your ancestral line does make a splash.

Rightly so, because your window on the world is wide open, filled with flashes of incredible insight. You look at a world filled with the opportunity to express yourself in the clearest of terms. No matter the obstacles presented, you overcome them with your will and refusal to be limited in your vision. "You accept the challenges so that you can feel the exhilaration of victory" (George S. Patton).

You are an original who sees the world in very different terms than most people. You have a deep emotional need to express your creativity in ways that touch the public consciousness. You change the thought patterns of the world through your unique accomplishments. You do stand out.

You can't be bound by traditional work methods or styles of living. You need space to allow your creative talents to blossom. Given periods of time away from the structures of society, you are allowed that room to explore.

Society sees you as unusual and different right from the get go. Even if they don't "get" you, you're still ready to go and do your own thing in your own way. Your daily lifestyle doesn't fit the pattern by which other people live; you operate outside the box.

Your success is based upon incredible intuition that guides your every move. Your mind is filled with possibilities and probabilities. You excel in any field you put your mind to because of your inventive ideas. Your physical presence sparks excitement and enthusiasm from the public. They never know what to expect next and that feeds the anticipation.

You explore the heavens, sing with the harmony of the spheres, pen messages for the ages, create red-carpet fashion, and lead righteous armies always in pursuit of the freedom of personal expression.

You are the cause for which you stand. Your presence speaks of the liberty needed for personal expression and progressive ideas which will be registered in the halls of memory to inspire future generations.

NEPTUNE SPEAKS TO COMPASSION, IMAGINATION, AND WISDOM

Neptune sesquiquintile Pluto:
This aspect happens rarely and rules blocks of generations. The most recent was 1941–1945. It will be exact again from 2040–2044. The allowable 3° orb expands the time periods.

This Generation's Legacy:
Transform society through spiritual awareness.

Discover this Generation's DNA Treasure:
This aspect does cover the latest generation who were born between 1941 and 1945.

Take another look at Grandma and Grandpa. These people were children when the atomic bomb was dropped on Nagasaki and Hiroshima, who grew up with the sound of hob-nailed boots on the pavement outside their homes by those who sought to destroy the "undesirables" in society. They grew up with the subconscious fears of their parents about monsters in the dark who were set on world domination and in whose hands were the weapons to wreak world destruction.

And yet . . . these people were inspired by compassion and gentleness and a firm belief in their faiths and the spirit of resurrection. Their acts of kindness in the midst of the horror of Plutonian destruction are recorded in the history books for all to read.

In this year 2018, those children born in the years around 1941–1945 are now in their seventies. These are the wise ones who have lived their lives with the knowledge of the evil that humans can do to one another, yet also with the knowledge of the spiritual goodness that shines through humans as well.

There are those among these seventy-year-olds, those who are firmly rooted in the mystical world of faith and the physical world of reality, who should be listened to because they have the key to transforming the world through spiritual compassion. If thoughts are things, as taught by metaphysicians through the ages and scientists have proven more recently, then we can learn from the dual worlds of this generation. Compassion and kindness walk hand-in-hand with the power of regeneration.

Mary Shelley, the author of *Frankenstein*, had this aspect. Her monster is a metaphor for the broken pieces of humanity sewn together to form a creature trying to function in normal society. The theme of her story, as one analyst writes, is that: "She is concerned with the use of knowledge for good or evil purposes . . . the treatment of the poor . . . and the restorative powers of nature in the face of unnatural events."

You, as the representative of your group, have a spiritual obligation to identify the hidden underbelly of society and to amass in groups to awaken the public to the absolute need for restructuring powerful institutions that seek to control body and soul. You are the Compassionate Transformer.

 **D³ ASC** **Neptune sesquiquintile Ascendant:**
Your Legacy:
Fog lights on high beam.

Discover Your DNA Treasure:
Built into your DNA is the Taoist parable posed by one of your ancestors: "Now I do not know whether I was then a man dreaming I was a butterfly, or whether I am now a butterfly, dreaming I am a man," so wrote Chinese philosopher Chuang-tzu after a dream.

When you wake up in the morning, you turn on your fog lights, the better to see your dream. Your great treasure in life is your sensitivity to your daily environment because it is through this lens that you speak to the world of love, compassion, and your brand of spirituality.

Where much of humanity walks around asleep, you peer into your dreams and see another reality. You live in two worlds. One is dreams, which are a source of inspiration from which you gain insight into human behavior. Your contribution to the pool of knowledge comes from your empathy and psychic understanding of human beings.

Your enormous creative talent endows you with an unlimited imagination. Your empathy for humanity shows in whatever life you choose to lead. You may explore the mystical side of life, preferring to live in serene places where you can connect with the spiritual side of life. Or you may find a home in the world of art through which you express your inner life. Or you may follow your heart's desire because you "have a dream."

You look at life as if through a dream. You know that . . . every blade of grass has its angel that bends over it and whispers, "grow, grow." (The Talmud) You see those angels.

There is something about you that intrigues the public. You have a subtle magnetism, a way of moving, that goes beyond your physical appearance. This is one of the qualities you possess that adds to the success of your mission.

You look at life as if through a dream. You know that . . . every blade of grass has sits angel that bends over it and whispers, "Grow, grow." (The Talmud) You see those angels.

Built into your DNA is a desire to contribute to the social commentary through your ability to see through the fog of public apathy, to remind the world that they should dream because dreams add meaning to life.

PLUTO SPEAKS TO FUNDAMENTAL TRANSFORMATION

♀ D³ ASC **Pluto sesquiquintile Ascendant:**
Your Legacy:
Lift the covers; open the blinds.

Discover Your DNA Treasure:
You come from a line of ancestors who opened the blinds to the world so that others could see. They knew that "who looks outside, dreams; who looks inside, awakes" (Carl Jung).

Just like your ancestors, you're here to lift the covers and peek underneath, to find out what's going on under there. There's no hidden agenda that you can't uncover. You are here to plumb the hidden terrains of human motivations and awaken humanity to their hidden motivations.

Through a basic motivational desire, you embrace nature in the eternal dance of procreation so that life will continue. Life, death, and transformation are the laws of life. You are here to transform society's sterile approach to all things creative.

Your intense view of life translates through everything you do. You see deeply into the hidden nature of others; your x-ray eyes penetrate the most casual conversation so there's no sense in others running because they can't hide from your penetrating mind.

You have the instincts of a detective with intense powers of concentration. You apply your intensity to solving problems. You search deep into cultural myths and become a voice for understanding amongst the belief systems of the world.

By exercising your talents through political insight and movements for fundamental change, you shed light in the darkness.

You are that light in the darkness, like the twelve-year-old French boy who changed the world of the blind through six bumps in various patterns spread out over a page. This boy capsulated Charles Barbier's "night writing" and the blind could read.

You raise public awareness of issues dealing with equality and sexuality. The Delta of Venus, originally marked as pornography in the 1940s, is today viewed as feminist pioneering work. You become the face of the feminist movement.

You believe that "possession isn't nine-tenths of the law. It's nine-tenths of the problem" (John Lennon). You set about to initiate, improve, and change the fundamental psychology of society, to be an example for a deeper look into the motivations that move human behavior. You are the catalyst for the tearing down of moldering structures and the resurrection of higher institutions of thought.

PART IV

TWO EXAMPLES

Wolfgang Amadeus
Mozart. *Courtesy the
Library of Congress.*

WOLFGANG AMADEUS MOZART

Wolfgang Amadeus Mozart, the youngest of seven children, was taught music by his father very early in his life. His father "insisted on a strong work ethic and perfection" (biography.com.

When Wolfgang was six, he was considered a prodigy and began his tour of Europe, performing before royalty in seventeen cities and seven different countries. Around age thirteen, after hearing Gregorio Allegri's *Miserere,* performed once in the Sistine Chapel, Wolfgang wrote the entire musical composition from memory, with only a few minor corrections.

In 1784, at age twenty-eight, Mozart had the most prolific period in his life. "During a five-week period, he appeared in twenty-two concerts, including five he produced and performed as a soloist" (biography.com).

On December 5, 1791, he died at age thirty-five, young even for that time period.

Mozart had the best-selling CD of 2016!

Mozart has:
Moon/Pluto in the 4th house quintile Venus in Aquarius in the 6th house. His deep emotional intensity was supported enthusiastically at home where he learned to apply his imagination to his work composing rapturous harmony in his unusual compositions. He performed to public acclaim as a child and through his youth.

He also has Mars quintile the Ascendant.

His Sun, Mercury, and Mars are sesquiquintile Jupiter, and Mars is sesquiquintile Uranus and quintile the Ascendant.

Loss of genius: The topic of *The Last Word* (*Week Magazine* , June 23, 2017) was: "Searching for the spark of genius." It reads: "Mozart's older sister Maria Anna, a brilliant harpsichordist, had her career cut short by her father when she reached the marriageable age of 18."

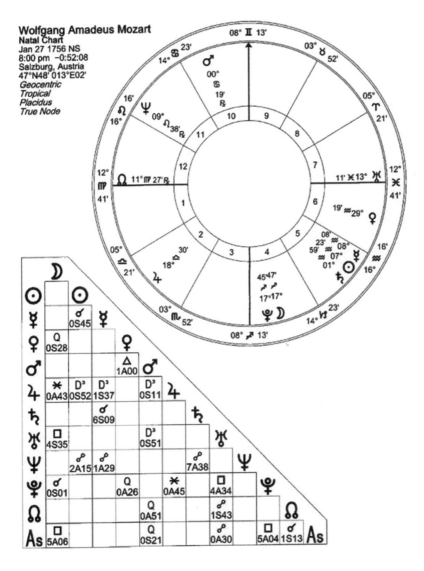

Rosa Parks.
*Courtesy the Library
of Congress.*

ROSA PARKS

On December 1, 1955, a soft-spoken forty-two-year-old black seamstress boarded a loaded bus after a long day's work. When told by the bus driver to give up her seat for a white man, she refused. Her action that day sparked the Montgomery Bus Boycott, which became a pivotal moment in the civil rights movement. She said later that she was pushed too far that day.

Among her many contributions, she was a member of the NAACP since 1943; she helped found the youth group in Montgomery where she taught young blacks to read so they could pass the literacy test in order to vote. She was involved in the legal movement to defend black women who were raped by white men, and she was a board member of Planned Parenthood of America in the 1980s.

Of her: Senator Marco Rubio said she was "an everyday American that changed the course of history." Senator Ted Cruz said she was "a principled pioneer that helped change this country."

She was aide to the Congressional office of US Representative John Conyer from 1964–1988. He said: "Rosa was a true giant of the civil rights movement. There are very few people who can claim their actions and conduct changed the face of the nation. Rosa Parks is one of those individuals."

In February 2013, a nine-foot bronze statue of Rosa Parks, known at the "mother of the Civil Rights movement" was unveiled in National Statuary Hall of the United States Capitol, one hundred years to the month of her birthday. The rock-like formation on which she is sitting seems a metaphor for her quiet unmovable determination. Spoken was the tribute: "…we celebrate a seamstress, slight of stature but mighty in courage." She was the first woman to be honored with a casket viewing in the Capitol Rotunda.

Rosa Parks has:
Mercury sesquiquintile Saturn, which describes her soft-spoken quiet refusal to give up her seat on the bus, a message that has reverberated through the last sixty years and will be her legacy for future generations, encouraging people to make their voices heard for just issues.

Her Venus in Aries quintile Mars and the Ascendant in Capricorn instilled in her the pioneering voice that would speak the message of equality for women and men to live in dignity. She fulfilled that in her lifetime as she rose in the Civil Rights movement and eventually held a respected position as an aide to a United States Congressman.

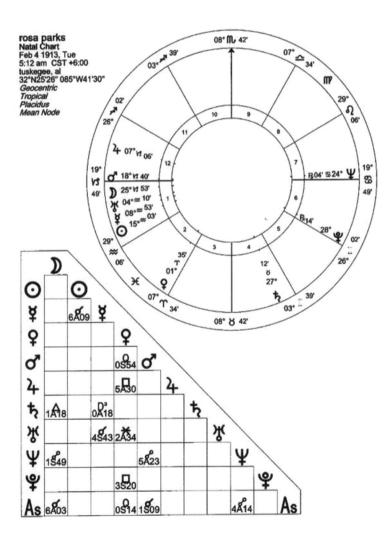

rosa parks
Natal Chart
Feb 4 1913, Tue
5:12 am CST +6:00
tuskegee, al
32°N25'26" 085°W41'30"
Geocentric
Tropical
Placidus
Mean Node

CONCLUSION

Well, there you have it, my friends. It's been quite a journey through the sands of time. I applaud you for hanging in here with me. I trust you have enjoyed the trek. I do hope you will continue to see numbers and geometrical shapes as languages that convey universal truths.

Samuel Taylor Coleridge, in his famous poem *The Rime of the Ancient Mariner*, wrote:

Water, water, every where, And all the boards did shrink.

Had he lived today, he might have written: Numbers, numbers, every where, and all the world does shrink.

The world has shrunk because of numbers. Numbers are not only the new language of global communication, they rule our lives. We are no longer face-to-face trading cows and pigs for the goods and services we need; we're more often behind an iPhone or a computer anonymously trading "invisible" cash for what we want. Our cash is out there somewhere, of course, but we don't see it. The trading is done through the binary language of the computer—zeroes and ones.

But . . . a number is a number is a number. From the moment of the Big Bang, on through the many trillions of years to the present and into the future, numbers are the one constant language that is dependable.

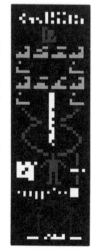

The Arecibo Message. Courtesy of Nasa.gov.

In fact, on November 16, 1974, SETI (Search for Extraterrestrial Intelligence) in Arecebo, Puerto Rico, sent a message from the largest radio telescope at that time toward the globular star cluster M13 some 25,000 light years away.

The first line of the message in binary code was the numbers 1 through 10! This was followed by the atomic number of the elements that make up the human body; then the makeup of our DNA. There was also a simplistic figure of a human along with the layout of our solar system. All this was done in the binary code of zeroes and ones.Scientists wanted to send a message to an alien intelligence and the first line of that message was our basic ten numbers!

And why is that? Because numbers are the universal language and the meaning of the numbers never change!

And in conclusion . . . you've heard that before—that usually means I'm not done, I have a lot more to say . . . but I can't help myself. I have to end with quotes from one of my treasured books, *Hermetic Masonry*, (1916) by Master Mason Frank C. Higgins. It's in two parts.

....

The Beginning of Masonry:

From the very beginning of things down to the 15th century, architecture is the great book of the human race . . . (p. 7)

In the fifteenth century all is changed—architecture is dethroned, the stone letters of Orpheus must give way to Gutenberg's letters of lead. (p. 10)

Almost all the ancient names of Deity, when their letters are resolved into numbers, are found to consist of what are sometimes called "cosmic" numbers, in that they set forth some great and majestic planetary or terrestrial cycle . . . (p. 41)

The Pi proportion is something that is never absent, in one form or other, from every one of the world's primitive religions, and certainly enters deeply and radically into the philosophies that have given rise to what we in these days call "Masonry." (p. 43)

The cube itself was an age-old symbol of the spiritual Man. (p. 55)

It will be discovered that some of the most important features of God's creation are inextricably built round the precise geometrical relation of a square to a circle. (p. 91)

Every number connected with our measurements of time is a "cosmic Number," . . . (p. 94)

Philology teaches us, however, that the word "God" is an old Turanian or Scythian word for "year," still surviving with its original meaning in the Slavonic Goda, a year. (p. 103)

The Lost Word:

All the ancient cosmogonies are geometrical projections beginning with the very first verse of the first chapter of Genesis where ALHIM (Elohim) the Pi proportion, creates the Heaven and the Earth. (p. 13)

The Egg was sacred to Isis and therefore the Priests of Egypt never ate eggs. (p. 38)

....

Now I'm done. Really.

You are now armed with two new languages with which to explore your world. Exercise those gray cells, create more wrinkles, and learn to think in these languages. They will open up a new world for you.

Thank you, dear reader, for spending this time with me. Take time to think today.

Love and Light . . .

END NOTES

PREHISTORY

1. From *Here On In*, reprinted in *Geocosmic New*, vol. 12, no. 1, fall 1987.

2. www.goodreads.com.

PART I

CHAPTER 1:
Preparation for Your Archaeological Expedition

1. Schwaller de Lubica, R. A., *The Temple in Man*, New York: Inner Traditions International, 1977, translated by Robert and Deborah Lawlor, translator's foreword, p. 10.

2. Voltaire, www.goodreads.com.

CHAPTER 2:
The Leader of This Expedition and His Treasure Map

1. Henricks, Robert G., *Lao Tzu's Tao Te Ching*, New York: Columbia University Press, 2000.

2. Lao Tzu, *Tao Te Ching*, from Carl Sagan, *Cosmos*, New York: Random House, 1980, p. 245.

3. Azimov, Isaac, *The Universe*, New York: Walker, 1908, pp. 210–211.

4. Sagan, Carl, *Cosmos*, New York: Random House, 1980, p. 246.

5. Ibid., p. 246.

CHAPTER 3:
Uncovering the Three from The Sands of Time

1. *Encyclopedia Americana*, Vol. 19, New York, Americana Corporation, 1966.

CHAPTER 4:
Uncovering the Four from The Sands of Time

1. www.billmoyers.com, Ep. 2: *Joseph Cambell and the Power of Myth.*

2. Higgins, Frank C., *Hermetic Masonry*, New York: Pyramid, 1916, p. 91.

CHAPTER 7:
Uncovering the Quintile and Sesquiquintile from The Sands of Time

1. Higgins, Frank C., *Hermetic Masonry*, New York: Pyramid, 1916, pp. 88–89.

CHAPTER 9:
The Pot of Gold

1. Higgins, Frank C., *Hermetic Masonry*, New York: Pyramid, 1916, p. 43.

PART II

CHAPTER 1:
The Natural Zodiac Technique and the Essence of the Houses

1. Hand, Robert, *Planets in Transit*, Gloucester, MA: Para Research, 1975, p. 19.

SUGGESTED READING LIST

Bunker, Dusty. *Numerology and Your Future*. West Chester, PA: Whitford Press, 1980.

Bunker, Dusty. *Numerology, Astrology, and Dreams*. West Chester, PA: Whitford Press, 1988.

Critchlow, Keith. *Time Stands Still*. New York: St. Martin's Press, 1982.

Doczi, Gyorgy. *The Power of Limits*. Boulder, CO: Shambhala Publications, Inc., 1981.

Gardner, Martin. *The Numerology of Dr. Matrix*. New York: Simon and Schuster, 1967.

Guthrie, Kenneth Sylvan (compiler and translator). *The Pythagorean Sourcebook and Library*. Grand Rapids, MI: Phanes Press, 1987.

Heline, Corinne. *Sacred Science of Numbers*. New Age Press, Inc., 1971. (Location unknown).

Henninger Jr., S. K. *Touches of Sweet Harmony: Pythagorean Cosmology and Renaissance Poetics*. San Marino, CA: The Huntington Library, 1974.

Higgins, Frank. *Hermetic Masonry*. New York: Pyramid Publishing Company, 1916; Ferndale MI: Trismegistus Press, 1980.

Huntley, H. E. *The Divine Proportion: A Study in Mathematical Beauty*. New York: Dover Publications, 1970.

Javane, Faith and Dusty Bunker. *Numerology and the Divine Triangle*. West Chester, PA: Whitford, Press, 1980.

The Lindisfarne Letter. "Geometry and Architecture." Vol. 10, West Stockbridge, MA: The Lindisfarne Association, 1980.

The Lindisfarne Letter, "Homage to Pythagoras." Vol. 14, West Stockbridge, MA: The Lindisfarne Association, 1980.

Oliver, George. *The Pythagorean Triangle*. (Part of the Secret Doctrine Reference Series). Wizard's Book Shelf, 1975.

Pennick, Nigel. *Sacred Geometry*. Wellingborough, Northamptonshire, England: Turnstone Press Limited, 1980.

Plummer, L. Gordon. *The Mathematics of the Cosmic Mind*. Wheaton IL: The Theosophical Publishing House, 1970.

Stebbing, Lionel. *The Secrets of Numbers*. London: New Knowledge Books, 1963.

Taylor, Thomas. *The Theoretic Arithmetic of the Pythagoreans*. New York: Samuel Weiser, 1978 (originally printed in London in 1816).

Tompkins, Peter. *Secrets of the Great Pyramid*. New York: Harper and Row, Inc., 1971.

Walker, Barbara. *The Woman's Encyclopedia of Myths and Secrets*. New York: Harper and Row, Inc., 1983, 46.

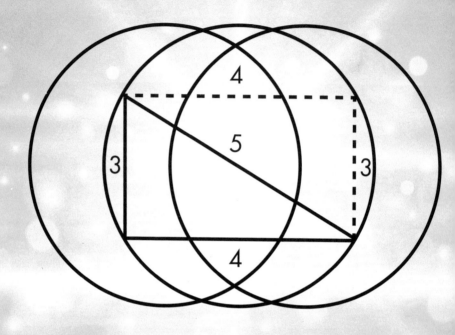

THE GOLDEN BOWL
RECTANGLE